"A LAMP'S ILLUMINATION" CONDENSED ADVICE ON GREAT COMPLETION'S THOROUGH CUT

by Dodrupchen III Tenpa'i Nyima

TONY DUFF
PADMA KARPO TRANSLATION COMMITTEE

First edition, January 2014
ISBN paper book: 978-9937-572-69-9
ISBN e-book: 978-9937-572-70-5

Janson typeface with diacritical marks and
Tibetan Classic Chogyal typeface
designed and created by Tony Duff,
Tibetan Computer Company
http://www.pktc.org/pktc

Produced, Printed, and Published by
Padma Karpo Translation Committee
P.O. Box 4957
Kathmandu
NEPAL

Committee members for this book: translation and composition, Tony Duff; cover design, Christopher Duff.

Web-site and e-mail contact through:
http://www.pktc.org/pktc
or search Padma Karpo Translation Committee on the web.

CONTENTS

INTRODUCTION

This book presents a text called *"A Lamp's Illumination" Condensed Advice on Great Completion's Thorough Cut*, written by the Tibetan master Jigmey Tenpa'i Nyima, the third Dodrupchen [1849–1907]. The text is an explanation of the Thorough Cut practice of innermost unsurpassed Great Completion.

Great Completion

The Great Completion system of dharma came from a land called Uddiyana, which is thought to have been in what is now the Swat region of Pakistan. The name of this system of dharma in the language of Uddiyana was "mahasandhi", meaning exactly "the great juncture". The Tibetans translated this name with "rdzogs pa chen po", which in English is "great completion". The words "juncture" and "completion" have the same meaning in this case; they refer to that one all-encompassing space, that one great juncture, in which all that there could be—whether enlightened or unenlightened, whether belonging to nirvana or samsara—is complete.

The name Great Completion refers both to an all-inclusive space that beings including humans could realize and to a system of instruction designed to bring beings to the realization of it[1]. When a being does realize it, there is nothing more to be realized or done because all is complete within that being's space of realization and the work of spiritual practice is complete. In a Buddhist way of talking, Great Completion is the final realization in which that being has manifested truly complete buddhahood.

Great Completion is often called "Great Perfection" in English but that presents an incorrect understanding of the name. The final space of realization is not a state of perfection but one that contains both perfection and imperfection. The name is not intended to connect us with the idea of perfection but with the idea of the juncture of all things perfect and imperfect, to the idea of a state of realization in which all things are complete.

There is also the unavoidable point that Longchen Rabjam's definitive explanations in his revered text *The Dharmadhatu Treasury* make it clear beyond a doubt that the meaning of the name is Great Completion and not Great Perfection. He mentions in several places that the point of the name is the inclusion—just as the original name from Uddiyana states—of all dharmas within a single unique sphere of wisdom.

Completion in the name means that all phenomena are included at once in a single space of realization. *Great* is used to distinguish something known by wisdom in direct perception from the same thing known by dualistic mind as a concept. Thus

---

[1] For realization, see the glossary.

Great Completion is not the completion understood through the use of concept, but the greater version of that, the actual state of completion known through wisdom. A second understanding of *great* is that Great Completion teaches the greatest level of completion of all Buddhist teachings; it points to the realization of a completion which is the greatest level of completion of all phenomena within the space of realization. Thus the term "greater completion" is also seen—for example in the text in this book—with the meaning that the Great Completion teaching teaches a greater level of completion than any of the teachings in the vehicles below it.

Levels of Great Completion Teaching

The Great Completion teaching is divided into three main sections, with each section being more profound than the previous one: Mind, Space, and Foremost Instruction sections. Of them, the Foremost Instruction section contains the most profound teaching of Great Completion. This section is sometimes further divided and sometimes not. When it is divided further, the most profound level of it has several names, the most common of which are "Nyingthig" meaning "quintessential" and "unsurpassed" and "innermost" Great Completion. This level of teaching is the most essential teaching of Great Completion—of reality—that has appeared in our current era of human society.

The text here is concerned with the Quintessential Great Completion teaching. This teaching has two main practices, one called Thorough Cut and one called Direct Crossing. This text concerns itself with Thorough Cut only.

Foremost Instructions

The Foremost Instruction section of the Great Completion teachings is given through what are called foremost instructions.

Many types of oral instruction are used in order to transmit the Buddhist teachings. Each has a style of its own and each is named accordingly. Unfortunately, the names of the various types of oral instruction have usually not been translated into English consistently or even correctly. Unfortunately because not doing so usually causes a major loss of understanding. For example, of these different types of oral instruction, there is one that is a key to understanding Quintessential Great Completion. It is the type of oral instruction called "upadesha" in the Sanskrit language. "Desha" means "verbal instruction", simple as that. "Upa" means the one above the others, the one that is better in every way, the one that comes at the front of all other types of instruction. It was translated into the Tibetan language with "man ngag", where *ngag* means the type of verbal instruction and *man* means the one that comes before all others. In English it is exactly, *foremost instruction*.

The particular quality of a foremost type of instruction is that it goes right to the heart of the person being instructed and connects the person very directly to the meaning being presented. It is not just a "pith" or "key" or "oral" instruction as so often translated but specifically is the foremost of all types of instruction, the one that has the ability to get right into and move the mind of the person who is being instructed.

The outstanding characteristic of the most profound teachings of Great Completion is that they are imparted not just with any kind of oral, pith, key or what-have-you instruction, but specifically with the *foremost* type of oral *instruction*.

Reading the Text of Tenpa'i Nyima's Teaching

This text, like most Tibetan texts, is not intended to be understood simply by reading the words. This needs to be said because, in the West especially, in modern times when there is a strong emphasis on education of the rational mind, there is a strong cultural habit of thinking that one should be able to pick up a book and read it and comprehend it. That is not the case here. This text can only function as a support for the oral instructions received from a qualified teacher with a lineage.

Supports for Study

Padma Karpo Translation Committee has amassed a range of materials that will assist the reader to understand the teachings in this text; see the chapter Supports for Study at the end of the book for the details.

Health Warning

The teaching of the text in this book is about a subject that is kept secret. Anyone who has had these teachings in person will be able to understand them or at least go to his teacher and ask for further explanation. Anyone who has heard these teachings in person from a qualified teacher, and especially who has had the introduction to the nature of mind upon which the teachings hinge, please use and enjoy the texts as you will. If you have not had a proper introduction to the nature of your mind, you would be better off not reading this book but seeking out someone who could teach it to you. In short, the contents of this book could be dangerous to your spiritual health if you are not ready for it, so exercise care.

With endless prostrations
To the Dodrupchen beings
And a constant stream of
Thanks to all of them!

Tony Duff,
Swayambunath,
Nepal,
January, 2014

"A LAMP'S ILLUMINATION"
CONDENSED ADVICE ON
GREAT COMPLETION'S THOROUGH CUT

by

DODRUPCHEN III TENPA'I NYIMA

I bow at the feet of the unequalled guru, the leader
    Vajradhara himself,
By whose kindness the reasoning connected with the
    supreme vehicle of Greater Completion
Was understood then faith in it gained.
That story retold here, something that will provoke
    joy in meditators,
Contains much about Great Completion.
It is a lamp that shows the picture of our own system
As championed by its charioteer, All-Knowing
    Longchenpa,
Which correctly illuminates but is highly condensed
    because
If much is said about this subject, it becomes a cause
    of argument.

1

It is best to sit quietly, not saying a word but
In order not to turn away from assisting those who
    pursue the meaning of dharma,
Automatically I have the idea to speak out and tell
    the king of tales.
Steered by the power of both authoritative statement
    and completely pure reasoning
I could explain it extensively, but steered by a
    shorter style
I am distilling this down to a short discussion of the
    key point of introduction,
In an explanation suited to those who take joy in
    condensed explanations.

Now, according to what the great champions of Great Completion's Foremost Instruction section accept, for this dharma you are: to train rational mind in the compassionate enlightenment mind[2]; to obtain completely the four empowerments elaborate, un-elaborate, and so on explained in the great *Sound Breakthrough*[3] then to keep the samayas as they should be kept; and especially, to obtain the transmission of blessings of the mind of the factual lineage[4] which makes the experience and realization of the vajra path come on abruptly. Note that they only accept that the transmission of blessings just referred to

---

[2] For enlightenment mind see the glossary.

[3] Tib. sgra thal 'gyur. This is the root tantra of the seventeen tantras which are the basis for the Foremost Instruction section of Great Completion.

[4] Factual is used in these texts to means the fact which can only be known beyond concept, by wisdom.

should be given to a disciple who is a suitable vessel, one who has the ability to please the master in many ways. They do not accept that this path is one without due process in which auspicious connection is put above all else, similar to a billet of wood in a cremation ground.[5]

In regard to that, there are those whose minds cannot, from the depths and without any pretense at all, stand to watch the great burden of suffering that is hard for all of the infinite sentient beings to carry and continuously attacks them in every moment. Because of that those people take delight in the prospect of attaining complete enlightenment as soon as possible, so they desire to accomplish it in this one life using this path to attain the rainbow body of great transference wisdom. They are the ones who have the capacity themselves to be a single captain who will liberate every single sentient being

---

[5] He is saying that the teaching itself, as shown by the great champions of the teaching, has due process. It does not allow for an immediate offering of the transmission of blessings to anyone with the justification that auspicious connection will take care of the avoidance of due process that then happens. This path has the process he has just laid out in four steps and disciples must go through that process from beginning to end. Not doing so would be similar to a billet of wood in the pyre used to cremate a person in an Indian cremation ground—it does not start fire at one end and gradually proceed to the other till it is fully ablaze, rather it catches alight all at once within the massive blaze of the funeral pyre. This is particularly relevant these days because it has become very popular for Tibetan lamas and even some Western ones to give the transmission-of-blessings introduction to people who have literally no understanding, preparation, or practice of this special path at all.

from samsara and they look without exception at what is dryly known by the name "the supreme vehicle, the king of vehicles".

To accomplish such a rank, they practise by joining the two paths of profound Thorough Cut and vast Direct Crossing, and it is necessary that they keep going until they have extracted the final experience. To begin with, they have to enter the first stage of those two trainings, the training in Thorough Cut, and it is that particular step that I will explain here.

The meaning of the name "Thorough Cut" is stated in the *Sound Breakthrough* to be that, through the power of doing Prajnaparamita meditation the appearances of grasped and grasping are simply cut right through. Prajnaparamita in this case is what is found at the level of having completely resolved the view as it is with—of the pair mind and rigpa—rigpa.

That rigpa is the view of actuality's own face. To obtain that view, first rigpa must be introduced and following that the method of placement[6] has to be one of preserving that rigpa without any contrivance of mind[7] That is the only way to obtain it; there is no need in the slightest for the references

---

[6] Method of placement is the means used when meditating—how one actually places the mind in the equipoise, as it is called, of meditation.

[7] Mind is dualistic mind, so it means "without the contrivances that are inherent to dualistic mind but are not part of rigpa".

and foci[8] that come with the elaborations "This activity is to be done" and "This meditation is to be done".

That is the practice, nevertheless it has been ascertained that before doing the practice it is necessary to receive the introduction to this rigpa using the steps stated in the tantra *Making the Introduction*. If that is not done beforehand, it will be difficult to see the dharmata nakedly, in the way that it is actually seated. Note though that, if the person being tamed by this process is someone who has trained his mindstream in this path in a previous life, he will not necessarily have to follow this sequence of steps for the introduction, for his situation is different from the others.

There are three parts to this introduction. The introduction to appearance as mind is that this object appearance which is shining forth as external facts for each of us now is for the yogin seen as a mere appearing factor of his internal mind. The introduction to mindness as empty is that this grasper which seems to be self-characterized[9] is moreover seen not to

---

[8] Referencing is the name for how conceptual mind operates and foci are the concepts themselves. Elaboration is the process of dualistic mind expressing thought and all of its other baggage. References and foci are elaborations. The method for placing yourself in rigpa, that is, the process of meditating on it, is completely exclusive of all dualistic approaches, including thinking "This is how I should go about it. Oh, I must meditate on it in this way".

[9] The grasper is the dualistic mind that apprehends the appearance mentioned in the first introduction. There are general and self-characterized phenomena. The former are the concepts,

(continued...)

exist in the slightest as an established thing. The introduction to being empty as rigpa is that all fictional appearances of object and its subject[10] are seen to be truthless, coming into appearance in the same way as illusions and dreams. That sequence of three introductions is what is to be trained in. It is a particular skilful means that gradually leads a certain type of person into the just thatness.

Nevertheless, there is also, within ultimate fact, an introduction to appearance as mind which does not require the dropping of clinging to truth. This was brought to light and explained by All-Knowing Jigmey Lingpa in accordance with what eminent Glorious Chandrakirti and All-Knowing Longchenpa accepted. This was done because of not agreeing with a differing classification of true and false made in regard to knower and knowable[11]. He pointed out that all of the

------

[9](...continued)
loosely stated, and the latter are actual phenomena which perform a function regardless of what is thought about them. In other words, you could say here "what seems to us to be the mind we have functioning internally and which seems truly to be an existent thing".

[10] The terms "object" and "subject" are literally "object" and "that which has an object". They refer to the object of some kind of awareness and the awareness which engages the object. Here, dualistic awarenesses, called consciousnesses, and their appearing objects are being referred to.

[11] To see the thread here, note that an object is a knowable and that which has the object, here called the subject, is a knower of that knowable.

appearances of the three realms and so on[12] are objects and their subjects coming as merely the self-lustre of thought and the energy of rigpa's liveliness for every one of which there is absolutely nothing to be found. By doing so, he exposed a fault present in the use of the convention "In relation to knowables there is a knower and in relation to a knower there is knowable" used to designate the two. The fault he exposed was that, using this designation, the two are being said to be false and nothing else. It has to be that the dhatu of luminosity-emptiness in which there is not so much as a speck of the fetters of grasping at the extremes of exists, does not exist, is, and is not is known using a personal, self-knowing rigpa. That has to be completely resolved and resolved with the certainty that it is not filled with mental mind that expresses that self-knowing as "other". Both are asserted in each level of intent of the tantras.[13]

---

[12] "And so on" means "nirvana". The samsaric appearances correspond to "self-lustre of thought" and the nirvanic ones correspond to "energy of rigpa's liveliness" mentioned immediately after this.

[13] This cannot be understood without knowing about self-empty and other-empty presentations of emptiness in Tibet. One tradition insisted that only self-emptiness as taught in the second turning of the wheel was the true teaching of Buddha. They correctly present emptiness in conjunction with interdependent origination. The convention mentioned in the paragraph comes from them. It is a statement of interdependency which by implication means that both subject and object are empty and therefore not existent. The advocates of this view in Tibet have historically been strongly and sometimes violently opposed to the presentation of what is called "other-emptiness taught in the third turning
(continued...)

Then, the main introduction is as follows. Generally speaking, many introductions that connect through example and meaning the twenty-one introductions, and so on—have been taught, but the central issue of the introduction in this case is met in the differentiation of mind and rigpa. Having seen this, the two all-knowing Ones used many approaches to pinpoint it and then explained it.

---

[13](...continued)
of the wheel of dharma". The Nyingmas, and Tenpa'i Nyima is one of them, accept self-emptiness but also accept other-emptiness. For them, simply to stop at empty interdependency is not enough, they need to present as really existing an awareness which every being has personally, and which has the unique feature of knowing itself, which includes all phenomena possible. Jigmey Lingpa, in presenting the highest level of Dzogchen teaching, pointed out that there was a way to have a direct introduction to reality, because everyone does have this awareness which is complete enlightenment in itself. It could be accessed by the main introduction, which is not one of the preliminary introductions shown above, that would directly show that kind of awareness, called rigpa, without having to engage in any dualistic mentality, such as one that would dualistically drop clinging. If you want to know more about this, our book *The Other Emptiness* explains the whole self-empty and other-empty subject to the point that this paragraph could be understood. The other topic here of introduction is mentioned in many of our other publications. The last sentence means that both self-empty and other-empty, not merely self-empty alone as that one tradition insists, are how reality has to be expressed and experienced, that both of them were the intent of the enlightened authors of the tantras. Again, the other tradition that prefers self-empty alone, has always cast the tantras in the light only of self-emptiness, but that is not what the tantras present.

Those who give little thought to looking at what is taught in the tantras concerning luminosity such as *Making the Introduction* which very precisely teach the difference between mind and rigpa through place, door, how they sit, and so on, and who do not consider the kindness of the differentiations made by foremost instruction, the meaning of the tantras, say that this "differentiation of mind and rigpa" was not known to the translators and pandits of the past but "was made up by Jigmey Lingpa himself". This ends up being nothing more than a lament of those pressed forward by maras of the mouth and is a bad omen for the tenets of the king of vehicles.

In that, the "mind" to be differentiated is as follows. The ordinary discursive thoughts which we now have—joy and sorrow, hope and fear, and so on—which have the character of being something other than it and the consciousnesses of the five doors that engage the grasped objects—all the conscious experiences of elaborating and abiding included in this and on its side—are only ever riders of the karmic winds. According to the example of this being an assemblage of a blind horse with legs and a rider with two eyes that glides along, it functions as the two of mind moving as an object and a grasper of the object, but[14] both All-Knowing Ones explained it as the capability of the wind-mind assemblage. In the tantra *Strings of Pearls* and others it is explained that the owner of becoming's creation and withdrawal is wind, but this is from considerations of many meanings connected with this here[15].

---

[14] … at the Great Completion Foremost Instruction level, which is being discussed here …

[15] … namely of Direct Crossing, but that is not the subject of this
(continued...)

It is not sufficient only to have identified mind, so if we continue our research, samsara without beginning happens due to the force of not rigpa[16]. And, from the ripening of latencies placed on one's own mindstream by karmic actions, a set of aggregates is appropriated and then, based on that, happiness and suffering arise like the prattling of a child. What happens next, the following along after the mind clinging to such, is demonstrated in the movements of mind clinging to ordinary confused appearances with outflows of place, body, possessions, and so on[17]. However much there is of that movement, all of it shines forth as being confused in double confusion because of being under the control of suddenly arising cause and effect, and then self-appearance is taken to be other appearance. If you think that there is no cause for the dye of confused appearance that alters the innate disposition of mind by confused appearance, you need to examine this further.

Moreover, persons who do not have the foremost instructions of a guru at the moment have not yet been introduced to the wisdom which is something other than and superior to this mind with its adventitiously-occurring objects. Nevertheless,

---

[15](...continued)
text, so he goes no further with it.

[16] The term "not rigpa" is usually translated as "ignorance". However, the original Sanskrit term "avidya" literally means "not rigpa" in contradistinction to rigpa and the pairing of terms is important in this presentation.

[17] Outflows, or more literally discharges from a sore, are what happens when wisdom loses its feet and a sore of not rigpa opens up and all of the samsaric stuff, including the ordinary appearances just mentioned, is discharged from it like pus.

in the system of this vehicle, that sort of inner wisdom primally has never known separation from the mindstream of all sentient beings, existing in them as the naked face itself of dharmakaya that will be shown by the guru's foremost instructions. After someone has recognized it with the aid of the guru's foremost instructions, this path has profound key points that will take the person further through the levels in a single ⋯⋯on of this path's equipoise than would happen by meditating for many aeons on the vipashyana of the other vehicles.

Briefly stated, there are three doorways that the guru can use to give the introduction to that wisdom as it actually sits. Due to its being seated as an empty entity, in not relating to grasping that happens with suppressing and furthering, it has never known the existence over the entity of so much as a speck of the fetters of mental analysis, so it is like a great wide-open vajra space. Due to its being seated as a luminosity nature, in not relating to the elaborating-withdrawing of removal-addition, it has never known entrance over the innate disposition of so much as a bit of the darkness of sinking and dullness, so it is like the vast disk of the luminous sun. Due to its being seated as all-pervading compassionate activity, in not relating to the weariness that comes with endeavours, it has never known accomplishment of confusion and liberation as something other than the self-liveliness of the innate, so it is like the dream of a great sleep. Now, in relation to each of those in order: rigpa's entity has alpha purity in that way, so the chance is there for the fruition of no-thought dharmakaya wisdom having the form of a pervasively spread emptiness to be accomplished; rigpa's nature has a factor of spontaneously-existing illumination in that way, so the chance is there for the fruition of sambhogakaya wisdom having the form of an unstopped lustre of the luminosity to shine forth as all superficies; rigpa's own liveliness has an all-pervasive compassionate activity in that way, so there is the chance for the nirmanakaya wisdom with its variety of play to arise in the form of appearance for those who are to be tamed.

Now, the empty primordial ground of the primal situation like that is not a blank annihilation, though it has no clinging to happiness. The luminosity of it is not shrouded by thought so is on show, cleaned out, sticking out. That, its character, is present in all beings as an element of precious gold that does not change into something else, but the three doors of ordinary people are wrapped up inside an enclosure having latencies, so in their case it does not see itself and remains just as the name "internalized luminosity, the youthful vase body".

If you enter the system of introduction over your own entity then follow on from that by making a decision over one thing and establishing assurance over liberation, you must be extremely careful[18]. There are indeed people who receive this introduction, whose roots of virtue are ripened because of it, and who because of that, when they meet the force of the abrupt transmission of blessings at the time of empowerments and so on, meet with wisdom[19]. However, in general, explana

---

[18] In other words, if you actually do this and get the introduction then do the two steps that follow as is explained in Garab Dorje's teaching *The Three Lines that Hit the Key Points*, you still have to be very careful in terms of how you proceed. It is very easy to take a wrong path in this system and the consequences can be disastrous.

[19] This is referring to people who already have significant training from the past. They are introduced, their roots of virtue from the

(continued...)

tions are given to the disciple using many spoken words and reasonings so that he can decide what it is really like, leading to the production of a very fine theoretical understanding that has him certain at that level of what it is really like. That is necessary and then, based on that theoretical understanding, it is necessary for him to keep practising with great perseverance for as long as he has not given rise to experience born of meditation—it is not enough for him merely to stay thinking, "This is view and meditation".

In short, the meaning of what is called "mind and wisdom" in this context should not be mixed up with its meaning when used in the other textual systems because there are extraordinary key points of the profound associated with that in this system. That wisdom can be made manifest now or it appears when ordinary sentient beings die. In the latter case, when all of the karmic winds have gathered into the space of the central channel, the wisdom appears for a moment as Samantabhadra's rigpa in full-view transparency without outside and inside, but is not identified at the time. In the former case, the yogin now, relying on the oral instructions of the method of placement, uses the system for making it manifest. What is that like? If you know how to preserve the wisdom explained immediately above based on recalling uncontrived dharmata as it actually is, then all of its liveliness's discursive thoughts—whether it has become attachment, aversion, or delusion—will

---

[19](...continued)

past are ripened, and then, when they attend such things as empowerments which contain the introduction, the introduction does not only give them a small glimpse of rigpa or perhaps even just a buzz, but actually opens wisdom, which is the fruition state of rigpa. This happens only to a very few people. Therefore ...

dissipate like clouds vanishing into dormancy in the state of the sky and then rigpa's entity will become clearer.

You might think, "Well then, what is the way of preserving wisdom's entity by recalling it?" For this many things have appeared in the tradition, such as the seven methods of placement and the three ways of liberation, and so on. However, their meaning in brief is that, having placed yourself initially in the previously introduced rigpa as exactly this ordinary discursive thought happening now, you stay in the recall of rigpa's entity without forgetting it even for a moment, which results in its stream being preserved. That procedure, moreover, is not one that has the vacillatory foci of recalled and recaller as with a target and an arrow. Rather, it is the face itself of the innate which merely by not being cast aside will bring a satisfied mind. Having done that, from within a spacious state of that mind at ease, there is the potential for the confusion of grasped-grasping to disintegrate directly; this is not merely taking count of how much thought is born and ceases but requires what meditators speak of as "looking directly at the entity of the thinker of the discursive thought that shines forth" or entrusting yourself to these very upsurges of rational mind.

In regard to doing meditation, dispelling the obstructors of experience has to be known and there are many of them to be known. However, the main point is that, if you become expert at severing sinking and agitation, dispelling obstructors will be for the most part complete within that. In regard to that, forceful strong binding of the mind results in the intensity of the knowing of rigpa being decreased and forceful loosening results in not being able to maintain the self-stationing of that mind. The severing of the two experiences of sinking and movement and the severing of the sinking that comes from rampant agitation with movement coming on in waves when you are distracted to objects is not done in this case with the concretizing type of mindfulness that goes with giving yourself hardship[20], like squeezing the mind into a box. Rather it is done with the mindfulness that automatically occurs within rigpa's own situation; with it, the intensity of the freshness is restored and the rigpa is re-energized, following which meditation on the rigpa can be resumed.

Now you might sever the rampant agitation, but you are still moving along in the double confusion of thought in general, such as "Abiding is good, movement is bad". Thus, there is something greater, higher than severing it, which is contact with the ultimate vanishing point of movement. For that, all engagements with rational mind are mixed into one-taste with rigpa, then, by placing yourself in that, everything that shines forth and appears as other than it, can only shine forth as the dharmakaya's play of liveliness. It is no longer possible for any of the thought to arise as an obstructor that could steal away the equipoise, so it becomes assurance of realization beyond the bias of self-liberation. This, which is called "all thoughts are the dharmakaya", is not even remotely like having some ordinary mind-experiences of shamatha in which a stable factor of abiding has been discovered and which some people refer to as "all thoughts are the dharmakaya". You can know

---

[20] From a Dzogchen perspective, giving yourself hardship—which in lesser vehicles means doing ascetic practice and the like—is not the way to proceed. Endeavour and striving only involves the use of a normal type of mindfulness, one which is restraining and which only serves to increase the already concrete situation of your samsaric existence.

more about this by looking at the commentary to *The Dharma-dhatu Treasury*[21].

Therefore, when you know this one faultless method of placement, you need to use its capability alone to cut sinking and agitation. This sort of dispelling of obstructors has no essence; it is like when many dogs have gathered together and are looking over at one dog, another can come from behind and carry the situation away.

In short, not having seen the profound key points of foremost instruction in which one hundred issues are wrapped up into one heading, but knowing only how to reach high within dharma terminology for words such as non-meditation, pervasive spread, and so on, does not bring any achievement of the levels at all, so you should become expert in the essential meaning of introduction and the method of placement.

> Experience has not happened in my mindstream,
> But due to having heard many foremost instructions
> of the lineage-holding guru,
> I have received hundreds of pure counsels such as
> "seeing the unseen".
> Due to the dharma conch at my throat bobbing up
> and down
> I have become a fool who values himself highly and
> Shows how brilliant he is due to his conceit of
> expertise, his philosopher's pride.
> Nevertheless, I have recorded in writing without
> fault the oral tradition

---

[21] This means Longchenpa's own commentary to it.

Of the previous vidyadharas whose speech was not
    adulterated with wanton gossip
As a key easy to understand and having an economy
    of expression.
Through understanding it the hundreds of locks on
    the excellent speech of the All-Knowing Ones
Will be opened wide for you after which you must
    through assiduous practice
Produce a special realization like a jewel coming to
    hand!
By the merit of having expressed in that way
The profound meaning foremost instruction's heart
    story,
May all of the infinite beings with a mind
Through relying on the narrow avenue of the vajra
    peak
Become buddha in the dhatu having six features[22].

After being urged for a long time by my tutor Dalpa Lodro Zangpo who always stationed himself nearby and also by the nun Tadrin who practices earnestly out of respect, I, Jigmey Tenpa'i Nyima, a crazy beggar from Dokham who is a mere reflection of an expounder of dharma, put this together in the practice centre Yalung Padma Kopa. May there be virtue and auspiciousness in all directions at all times. Virtue! Virtue! Virtue!

---

[22] "Dhatu" here is the dharmadhatu in the form of the fruitional youthful vase body, which in the Foremost Instruction section of Great Completion is described as having six features.

GLOSSARY OF TERMS

Actuality, Tib. gnas lugs: A key term in both sūtra and tantra and one of a pair of terms, the other being "apparent reality" (Tib. snang lugs). The two terms are used when determining the reality of a situation. The actuality of any given situation is how (lugs) the situation actuality sits or is present (gnas); the apparent reality is how (lugs) any given situation appears (snang) to an observer. Something could appear in many different ways, depending on the circumstances at the time and on the being perceiving it but, regardless of those circumstances, it will always have its own actuality of how it really is. This term is frequently used in Mahāmudrā and Great Completion teachings to mean the fundamental reality of any given phenomenon or situation before any deluded mind alters it and makes it appear differently.

Adventitious, Tib. glo bur: This term has the connotations of popping up on the surface of something and of not being part of that thing. Therefore, even though it is often translated as "sudden", that only conveys half of the meaning. In Buddhist literature, something adventitious comes up as a surface event and disappears again precisely because it is not actually part of the thing on whose surface it appeared. It is frequently used in relation to the afflictions because they pop up on the surface of the mind of buddha-nature but are not part of the buddha-nature itself.

All-Knowing One, Tib. kun mkhyen: Every century in Tibet, there were just a few people who seemed to know everything so were given the title "All-Knowing One". In this text it is used to refer both to Longchen Rabjam and Jigmey Lingpa. Note that "All-Knowing" does not mean "omniscient one" even though it is often translated that way.

Alpha purity, Tib. ka dag: A Great Completion term meaning purity that is there from the first, that is, primordial purity. There are many terms in Buddhism that express the notion of "primordial purity" but this one is unique to the Great Completion teaching. The term "alpha purity" matches the Tibetan term both literally and in meaning.

Appropriation, Skt. upādāna, Tib. nye bar len pa: This is the name of the ninth of the twelve links of interdependent origination. Tsongkhapa gives a good treatment of all twelve links in his interdependent origination section of the *Great Stages of the Path to Enlightenment*, a translation of which is available for free download from the PKTC web-site. It is the crucial point in the process at which a karma that has been previously planted is selected and activated as the karma that will propel the being into its next existence. In other words, it is the key point in a being's existence when the next type of existence is selected. There is the further point that, at the time of death, the particular place that the wind-mind settles in the subtle body, a place related to the seed syllables mentioned in the tantras, also determines the next birth. The two points are not different. The selection of the karma that will propel the next life then affects how the wind-mind will operate at the time of death.

Assurance, Tib. gdeng: Although often translated as confidence, this term means assurance with all of the extra meaning conveyed by that term. A bird might be confident of its ability to fly but, more than that, it has the assurance that it will not fall to the ground because it knows it has wings and it has the training to use them. Similarly, a person might be confident that he could liberate the afflictions but not be assured of doing so because of lack of training or other causes. However, a person who has accumulated the causes to be able to liberate afflictions is assured of the ability to do so.

Authoritative statement, Skt. āgama, Tib lung: Although often translated as "scripture", authentic statement means statement made by someone who has the true knowledge needed to make fully reliable statements about a subject. It is often used to indicate dharma taught by the Buddha or his disciples which is authoritative because of its source. It is also used in the pair "authoritative statement and realization" which, the Buddha explained, summed up the ways of transmitting his realization.

Awareness, Skt. jñā, Tib. shes pa: "Awareness" is always used in our translations to mean the basic knower of mind or, as Buddhist teaching itself defines it, "a general term for any registering mind", whether dualistic or non-dualistic. Hence, it is used for both samsaric and nirvanic situations; for example, consciousness (Tib. rnam par shes pa) is a dualistic form of awareness, whereas rigpa, wisdom (Tib. ye shes), and so on are non-dualistic forms of awareness. See under rigpa.

It is noteworthy that the key term "rigpa" is often mistakenly translated as "awareness", even though it is not merely an awareness; this creates considerable confusion amongst practitioners of the higher tantras who are misled by it.

Becoming, Skt. bhāvanā, Tib. srid pa: This is another name for samsaric existence. Beings in saṃsāra have a samsaric existence but, more than that, they are constantly in a state of becoming—becoming this type of being or that type of being in this abode or that, as they are driven along without choice by the karmic process that drives samsaric existence.

Clinging, Tib. zhen pa: In Buddhism, this term refers specifically to the twofold process of dualistic mind mis-taking things that are not true, not pure, as true, pure, etcetera and then, because of seeing them as highly desirable even though they are not, attaching itself to or clinging to those things. This type of clinging acts as a kind of glue that keeps a person joined to the unsatisfactory things of cyclic existence because of mistakenly seeing them as desirable.

Compassionate activity, Tib. thugs rje: This does not mean compassionate activity in general. Rather, it is a specific term of the most profound level of teachings of Mahāmudrā and Great Completion. These teachings describe innate wisdom as having three characteristics. The third characteristic is this compassionate activity. It refers to the fact that wisdom spontaneously does whatever needs to be done, throughout all reaches of time and space, for all beings. Although it includes the word "compassion" in its name, it is more primordial than that. It is the dynamic quality of enlightenment which choicelessly, ceaselessly, spontaneously, and pervasively acts to benefit others. The term is often used in discussions of Great Completion and essence Mahāmudrā.

Concretization, Tib. a 'thas: This is a very strong term that has the full weight of "the deep stupidity of ignorance which solidifies empty actuality into concrete existence". This is how samsaric mind operates. It does not merely live in dualistic ways of knowing but solidifies all that it knows into the perception of a very concrete existence.

Confusion, Tib. 'khrul pa: In Buddhism, this term mostly refers to the fundamental confusion of taking things the wrong way that happens because of fundamental ignorance, although it can also have the more general meaning of having lots of thoughts and being confused about it. In the first case, it is defined like this "Confusion is the appearance to rational mind of something being present when it is not" and refers,

for example, to seeing an object, such as a table, as being truly
present, when in fact it is present only as mere, interdependent appearance.

Consciousness, Skt. vijñāna, Tib. rnam shes: The term means
"awareness of superficies". A consciousness is a dualistic (jñā)
awareness which simply registers a certain type of (vi) superfice, for example, an eye consciousness by definition registers
only the superficies of visual form. A very important point is
that the addition of the "vi" to the basic term (jñā) for awareness conveys the sense of a less than perfect way of being
aware. This is not a wisdom awareness which knows every
superfice in an utterly uncomplicated way but a limited type
of awareness which is restricted to knowing one kind of
superfice or another and which is part of the complicated—
and highly unsatisfactory process—called (dualistic) mind.
Note that this definition, which is a crucial part of understanding the role of consciousness in samsaric being, is fully
conveyed by the Sanskrit and Tibetan terms but not at all by
the English term.

Contrivance, contrived, Tib. bcos pa: A term meaning that something has been altered from its native state.

Cyclic existence: See under saṃsāra.

Dharmadhatu, Skt. dharmadhātu, Tib. chos kyi dbyings: A *dhātu*
is a place or basis from or within which something can come
into being. In the case of a dharma dhātu, it is the place or
space which is a basis from and in which all dharmas or
phenomena, can and do come into being. If a flower bed is
the place where flowers grow and are found, the dharmadhātu is the dharma or phenomena bed in which all phenomena come into being and are found. The term is used in all
levels of Buddhist teaching with that general meaning but the
explanation of it becomes more profound as the teaching
becomes more profound. For example, in Great Completion
and Mahāmudrā, it is the all-pervading sphere of luminosity-

wisdom, given that luminosity is where phenomena arise and luminosity is none other than wisdom.

Dharmakaya, Skt. dharmakāya, Tib. chos sku: In the general teachings of Buddhism, this refers to the mind of a buddha, with "dharma" meaning reality and "kāya" meaning body. In the Thorough Cut practice of Great Completion it additionally has the special meaning of being the means by which one rapidly imposes liberation on oneself.

Dharmata, Skt. dharmatā, Tib. chos nyid: This is a general term meaning the way that something is, and can be applied to anything at all; it is similar in meaning to "actuality" *q.v.* For example, the dharmatā of water is wetness and the dharmatā of the becoming bardo is a place where beings are in a samsaric, or becoming mode, prior to entering a nature bardo. It is used frequently in Tibetan Buddhism to mean "the dharmatā of reality" but that is a specific case of the much larger meaning of the term. To read texts which use this term successfully, one has to understand that the term has a general meaning and then see how that applies in context.

Direct Crossing, Tib. thod rgal: The name of one of the two main practices of the innermost level of Great Completion. The other one is Thorough Cut *q.v.*

Discursive thought, Skt. vikalpa, Tib. rnam rtog: This means more than just the superficial thought that is heard as a voice in the head. It includes the entirety of conceptual process that arises due to mind contacting any object of any of the senses. The Sanskrit and Tibetan literally mean "(dualistic) thought (that arises from the mind wandering among the) various (superficies *q.v.* perceived in the doors of the senses)".

Elaboration, Tib. spro ba: This is a general name for what is given off by dualistic mind as it goes about its conceptual business. The term is pejorative in that it implies that a story has been made up, un-necessarily, about something which is actually nothing, which is empty. Elaborations, because of what they are, prevent a person from seeing emptiness directly.

Freedom from elaboration or being elaboration-free implies direct sight of emptiness. It is important to understand that these words are used in a theoretical or philosophical way in the second turning sūtra teachings but are used in an experiential way in the final teachings of the third turning sūtras and in the tantras of Great Completion and Mahāmudrā. In the former, being free of elaborations is a definition of what could happen according to the tenets of the Middle Way, and so on; in the latter it is a description of a state of being, one which, because it is empty of all the elaborations of dualistic being, is the actual sphere of emptiness.

Enlightenment mind, Skt. bodhicitta, Tib. byang chub sems: This is a key term of the Great Vehicle. It is the type of mind that is connected not with the lesser enlightenment of an arhat but the enlightenment of a truly complete buddha. As such, it is a mind which is connected with the aim of bringing all sentient beings to that same level of buddhahood. A person who has this mind has entered the Great Vehicle and is either a bodhisatva or a buddha.

It is important to understand that "enlightenment mind" is used to refer equally to the minds of all levels of bodhisatva on the path to buddhahood and to the mind of a buddha who has completed the path. Therefore, it is not "mind striving for enlightenment" as is so often translated, but "enlightenment mind", meaning that kind of mind which is connected with the full enlightenment of a truly complete buddha and which is present in all those who belong to the Great Vehicle.

Entity, Tib. ngo bo: The entity of something is just exactly what that thing is. In English we would often simply say "thing" rather than entity. However, in Buddhism, "thing" has a very specific meaning rather than the general meaning that it has in English. It has become common to translate this term as "essence" *q.v.* However, in most cases "entity", meaning what a thing is rather than an essence of that thing, is the correct translation for this term.

Fact, Skt. artha, Tib. don: "Fact" is that knowledge of an object that occurs to the surface of mind or wisdom. It is not the object but what the mind or wisdom understands as the object. Thus there are two usages of "fact": fact known to dualistic and non-dualistic minds. The higher tantras especially use "fact" to refer to the actual fact known in direct perception of actuality. Thus, there are phrases such as "in fact" which do not mean that the author is speaking truly about something but that whatever is about to be said is referring to actual fact as known to wisdom. A further complexity is that phrases such as "in fact" in those contexts are often abbreviations of "in superfact" *q.v.* This brings a further difficulty for the reader because "superfact" can be used in a general way to indicate directly perceived non-samsaric fact or can be used according to its specific definition (for which see superfact). In Buddhist tradition, problems like this are solved by having the text explained by one's teacher. That might not be possible for some readers, so uses of the word "fact" should be looked at carefully to see whether they are indicating fact in general or the factual situation of knowing reality in direct perception.

Fictional, Skt. saṃvṛtti, Tib. kun rdzob: This term is paired with the term "superfactual" *q.v.* In the past, these terms have been translated as "relative" and "absolute" respectively, but those translations are nothing like the original terms. These terms are extremely important in the Buddhist teaching so it is very important that they be corrected, but more than that, if the actual meaning of these terms is not presented, then the teaching connected with them cannot be understood.

The Sanskrit term saṃvṛtti means a deliberate invention, a fiction, a hoax. It refers to the mind of ignorance which, because of being obscured and so not seeing suchness, is not true but a fiction. The things that appear to that ignorance are therefore fictional. Nonetheless, the beings who live in this ignorance believe that the things that appear to them through the filter of ignorance are true, are real. Therefore, these beings live in fictional truth.

Fictional and superfactual: Fictional and superfactual are our greatly improved translations for "relative" and "absolute" respectively. Briefly, the original Sanskrit word for fiction means a deliberately produced *fiction* and refers to the world projected by a mind controlled by ignorance. The original word for superfact means "that *superior fact* that appears on the surface of the mind of a noble one who has transcended saṃsāra" and refers to reality seen as it actually is. Relative and absolute do not convey this meaning at all and, when they are used, the meaning being presented is simply lost.

Foci, focus, focus on, Tib. gtad so: A focus is any given thing that a dualistic mind has focussed on. Having a focus is equivalent to having a reference *q.v.*, and focussing on a focus entails referencing a reference. All of these terms imply the presence of dualistic mind.

Foremost instruction, Skt. upadeśha, Tib. man ngag: There are several types of instruction mentioned in Buddhist literature: there is the general level of instruction which is the meaning contained in the words of the texts of the tradition; on a more personal and direct level there is oral instruction which has been passed down from teacher to student from the time of the buddha; and on the most profound level there are foremost instructions which are not only oral instructions provided by one's guru but are special, core instructions that come out of personal experience and which convey the teaching concisely and with the full weight of personal experience. Foremost instructions or upadeśha are crucial to the Vajra Vehicle because these are the special way of passing on the profound instructions needed for the student's realization.

Grasped-grasping, Tib. gzung 'dzin: When mind is turned outwardly as it is in the normal operation of dualistic mind, it has developed two faces that appear simultaneously. Special names are given to these two faces: mind appearing in the form of the external object being referenced is called "that which is grasped" and mind appearing in the form of the consciousness that is registering it is called the "grasper" or "grasping" of it. Thus, there is the pair of terms "grasped-grasper" or "grasped-grasping". When these two terms are used, it alerts one to the fact that a Mind Only style of presentation is being discussed. This pair of terms pervades Mind Only, Middle Way, and tantric writings and is exceptionally important in all of them.

Note that one could substitute the word "apprehended" for "grasped" and "apprehender" for "grasper" or "grasping" and that would reflect one connotation of the original Sanskrit terminology. The solidified duality of grasped and grasper is nothing but an invention of dualistic thought; it has that kind of character or characteristic.

Illumination, Skt. vara, Tib. gsal ba: This term should be understood as an abbreviation of the Tibetan term, "'od gsal ba", which is translated with luminosity *q.v.* Illumination is not another factor of mind distinct from luminosity but merely a convenient abbreviation for it.

Intent, Tib. dgongs pa: This is the honorific form of (Tib. sems pa) meaning "to think, to comprehend", so is used to refer to an enlightened person's understanding, though the Gelugpa school is even more restrictive and uses it only for wisdom understanding of the Buddha. In some places "intent" meaning the intended meaning based on an enlightened person's understanding and in other places simply "understanding" should be understood for this term.

Introduction and To Introduce, Tib. ngos sprad and ngos sprod pa respectively: This pair of terms is usually mistakenly translated today as "pointing out" and "to point out. The terms are the standard terms used in day to day life for the situation in which one person introduces another person to someone or something. They are the exact same words as our English "introduction" and "to introduce".

In the Vajra Vehicle, these terms are specifically used for the situation in which one person introduces another person to the nature of his own mind. There is a term in Tibetan for "pointing out", but that term is never used for this purpose because in this case no one points out anything. Rather, a person is introduced by another person to a part of himself that he has forgotten about.

Kaya, Skt. kāya, Tib. sku: The Sanskrit term means a functional or coherent collection of parts, similar to the French "corps", and hence also comes to mean "a body". It is used in Tibetan Buddhist texts specifically to distinguish bodies belonging to the enlightened side from ones belonging to the samsaric side.

Enlightened being in Buddhism is said to be comprised of one or more kayas. It is most commonly explained to consist of one, two, three, four, or five kāyas, though it is pointed out that there are infinite aspects to enlightened being and therefore it can also be said to consist of an infinite number of kāyas. In fact, these descriptions of enlightened being consisting of one or more kāyas are given for the sake of understanding what is beyond conceptual understanding so should not be taken as absolute statements.

The most common description of enlightened being is that it is comprised of three kāyas: dharma, saṃbhoga, and nirmāṇakāyas. Briefly stated, the dharmakāya is the body of truth, the saṃbhogakāya is the body replete with the good qualities of enlightenment, and the nirmāṇakāya is the body manifested into the worlds of saṃsāra and nirvāṇa to benefit beings.

Dharmakāya refers to that aspect of enlightened being in which the being sees the truth for himself and, in doing so, fulfils his own needs for enlightenment. The dharmakāya is purely mind, without form. The remaining two bodies are summed up under the heading of rūpakāyas or form bodies manifested specifically to fulfil the needs of all un-enlightened beings. "Saṃbhogakāya" has been mostly translated as "body of enjoyment" or "body of rapture" but it is clearly stated in Buddhist texts on the subject that the name refers to a situation replete with what is useful, that is, to the fact that the saṃbhogakāya contains all of the good qualities of enlightenment as needed to benefit sentient beings. The saṃbhogakāya is extremely subtle and not accessible by most sentient beings; the nirmāṇakāya is a coarser manifestation which can reach sentient beings in many ways. Nirmāṇakāya should not be thought of as a physical body but as the capability to express enlightened being in whatever way is needed throughout all the different worlds of sentient beings. Thus, as much as it appears as a supreme buddha who shows the dharma to beings, it also appears as anything needed within sentient beings' worlds to give them assistance.

The three kāyas of enlightened being is taught in all levels of Buddhist teaching. It is especially important in Mahāmudrā and Great Completion and is taught there in a unique and very profound way.

Key points, Tib. gnad: Key points are those places in one's being that one works, like pressing buttons, in order to get some desired effect. For example, in meditation, there are key points of the body; by adjusting those key points, the mind is brought closer to reality and the meditation is thus assisted.

In general, this term is used in Buddhist meditation instruction but it is, in particular, part of the special vocabulary of the Great Completion teachings. Overall, the Great Completion teachings are given as a series of key points that must be attended to in order to bring forth the various realizations of the path.

Latency, Skt. vāsanā, Tib. bag chags: The original Sanskrit has the meaning exactly of "latency". The Tibetan term translates that inexactly with "something sitting there (Tib. chags) within the environment of mind (Tib. bag)". Although it has become popular to translate this term into English with "habitual pattern", that is not its meaning. The term refers to a karmic seed that has been imprinted on the mindstream and is present there as a latency, ready and waiting to come into manifestation.

Liveliness, Tib. rtsal: This is a key term in both Mahāmudrā and Great Completion. The term is sometimes translated as "display" or "expression" but neither is correct. The primary meaning is the ability of something to express itself but in use, the actual expression of that ability is also included. Thus, in English it would not be "expression" but "expressivity" but that is too dry. This term is not at all dry; it is talking about the life of something and how that life comes into expression; "liveliness" fits the meaning of the original term very well.

Luminosity, Skt. prabhāsvara, Tib. 'od gsal ba: The core of mind has two aspects: an emptiness factor and a knowing factor. The Buddha and many Indian religious teachers used "luminosity" as a metaphor for the knowing quality of the core of mind. If in English we would say "Mind has a knowing quality", the teachers of ancient India would say, "Mind has an illuminative quality; it is like a source of light which illuminates what it knows".

This term has been translated as "clear light" but that is a mistake that comes from not understanding the etymology of the word. It does not refer to a light that has the quality of clearness (something that makes no sense, actually!) but to the illuminative property which is the nature of the empty mind.

Note also that in both Sanskrit and Tibetan Buddhist literature, this term is frequently abbreviated just to Skt. "vara" and Tib. "gsal ba" with no change of meaning. Unfortunately, this has been thought to be another word and it has then been translated with "clarity", when in fact it is just this term in abbreviation.

Lustre, Tib. mdangs: In both Mahāmudrā and Great Completion there is the general term "gdangs" meaning what is given off or emitted by something in general, for example the sound given off by a loudspeaker or what the empty factor of mind emits. The Mahāmudrā teaching does not distinguish between "gdangs" and "mdangs" but the Great Completion teaching does. In Great Completion, this term has the more refined meaning of the "complexion" or "lustre" of thing. In this teaching, there is the "gdangs" output of the empty aspect of mind in general, but there is also the more subtle "mdangs" complexion or lustre which is an aspect of the output of that emptiness.

Mara, Skt. māra, Tib. bdud: The Sanskrit term is closely related to the word "death". Buddha spoke of four classes of extremely negative influences that have the capacity to drag a sentient being deep into saṃsāra. They are the "maras" or "kiss of death": of having a samsaric set of five skandhas; of having afflictions; of death itself; and of the son of gods, which means being seduced and taken in totally by sensuality.

Mind, Skt. chitta, Tib. sems: There are several terms for mind in the Buddhist tradition, each with its own, specific meaning. This term is the most general term for the samsaric type of mind. It refers to the type of mind that is produced because of fundamental ignorance of enlightened mind. Whereas the wisdom of enlightened mind lacks all complexity and knows in a non-dualistic way, this mind of un-enlightenment is a very complicated apparatus that only ever knows in a dualistic way.

Mindness, Skt. chittatā, Tib. sems nyid: Mindness is a specific term of the tantras. It is one of many terms meaning the essence of mind or the nature of mind. It conveys the sense of "what mind is at its very core". It has sometimes been translated as "mind itself" but that is a misunderstanding of the Tibetan word "nyid". The term does not mean "that thing mind" where mind refers to dualistic mind. Rather, it means the very core of dualistic mind, what mind is at root, without all of the dualistic baggage.

Mindness is a path term. It refers to exactly the same thing as "actuality" or "actuality of mind" which is a ground term but does so from the practitioner's perspective. It conveys the sense to a practitioner that he has baggage of dualistic mind that has not yet been purified but that there is a core to that mind that he can work with.

Not rigpa, Skt. avidya, Tib. ma rig pa: Rigpa *q.v.* is a key term in these discussions. It refers to the enlightened kind of knowing. Its opposite, not-rigpa, which refers to the unenlightened way of knowing, is equally important. As it says in the *Abhidharmakosha*, "not-rigpa is not merely a discordance with rigpa but is its very opposite". Not-rigpa is usually translated as ignorance but this masks the all-important opposing relationship between rigpa and not-rigpa. Therefore, in this book, this term is usually translated as "not-rigpa" rather than "ignorance".

Output, Tib. gdangs: Output is a general term for that which is given off by something, for example, the sound that comes from a loudspeaker. In Mahāmudrā and Great Completion, it refers to what is given off by the emptiness factor of the essence of mind. Emptiness is the empty condition of the essence of mind, like space. However, that emptiness has liveliness which comes off the emptiness as compassion and all the other qualities of enlightened mind, and, equally, all the apparatus of dualistic mind. All of this is called its output. Note that the Great Completion teachings have a special word that is a more refined version of this term; see under lustre for that.

Outflow, Skt. āsrāva, Tib. zag pa: The Sanskrit term means a bad discharge, like pus coming out of a wound. Outflows occur when wisdom loses its footing and falls into the elaborations of dualistic mind. Therefore, anything with duality also has outflows. This is sometimes translated as "defiled" or "conditioned" but these fail to capture the meaning. The idea is that wisdom can remain self-contained in its own unique sphere but, when it loses its ability to stay within itself, it starts to have leakages into dualism that are defilements on the wisdom. See also under un-outflowed.

Preserve, Tib. skyong ba: This term is important in both Mahāmudrā and Great Completion. In general, it means to defend, protect, nurture, maintain. In the higher tantras it means to keep something just as it is, to nurture that something so that it stays and is not lost. Also, in the higher tantras, it is often used in reference to preserving the state where the state is some particular state of being. Because of this, the phrase "preserve the state" is an important instruction in the higher tantras.

Rational mind, Tib. blo: Rational mind is one of several terms for mind in Buddhist terminology. It specifically refers to a mind that judges this against that. With rare exception it is used to refer to samsaric mind, given that samsaric mind only works in the dualistic mode of comparing this versus that. Because of this, the term is mostly used in a pejorative sense to point out samsaric mind as opposed to an enlightened type of mind.

The Gelugpa tradition does have a positive meaning for this term and their documents will sometimes use it in that way;

they make the claim that a buddha has an enlightened type of this mind. That is not wrong; one could refer to the ability of a buddha's wisdom to make a distinction between this and that with the term "rational mind". However, the Kagyu and Nyingma traditions in their Mahāmudrā and Great Completion teachings, reserve this term for the dualistic mind. In their teachings, it is the villain, so to speak, which needs to be removed from the practitioner's being in order to obtain enlightenment.

This term has been commonly translated simply as "mind" but that fails to identify this term properly and leaves it confused with the many other words that are also translated simply as "mind". It is not just another mind but is specifically the sort of mind that creates the situation of this and that (*ratio* in Latin) and hence, at least in the teachings of Kagyu and Nyingma, upholds the duality of saṃsāra. In that case, it is the very opposite of the essence of mind. Thus, this is a key term which should be noted and not just glossed over as "mind".

Realization, Tib. rtogs pa: Realization has a very specific meaning: it refers to correct knowledge that has been gained in such a way that the knowledge does not abate. There are two important points here. Firstly, realization is not absolute. It refers to the removal of obscurations, one at a time. Each time that a practitioner removes an obscuration, he gains a realization because of it. Therefore, there are as many levels of realization as there are obscurations. Maitreya, in the *Ornament of Manifest Realizations*, shows how the removal of the various obscurations that go with each of the three realms of samsaric existence produces realization.

Secondly, realization is stable or, as the Tibetan wording says, "unchanging". As Guru Rinpoche pointed out, "Intellectual knowledge is like a patch, it drops away; experiences on the path are temporary, they evaporate like mist; realization is unchanging".

A special usage of "realization" is found in the Essence Mahāmudrā and Great Completion teachings. There, realization is the term used to describe what happens at the moment when mindness is actually met during either introduction to or self-recognition of mindness. It is called realization because, in that glimpse, one actually directly sees the innate wisdom mind. The realization has not been stabilized but it is realization.

Reference and Referencing, Tib. dmigs pa: Referencing is the name for the process in which dualistic mind references an actual object by using a conceptual label instead of the actual object. Whatever is referenced is then called a reference. Note that these terms imply the presence of dualistic mind and their opposites, non-referencing and being without reference imply the presence of non-dualistic wisdom.

Rigpa, Tib. rig pa: This is the singularly most important term in the whole of Great Completion and Mahāmudrā. In particular, it is the key word of all words in the Great Completion system of the Thorough Cut. Rigpa literally means to know in the sense of "I see!" It is used at all levels of meaning from the coarsest everyday sense of knowing something to the deepest sense of knowing something as presented in the system of Thorough Cut. The system of Thorough Cut uses this term in a very special sense, though it still retains its basic meaning of "to know". To translate it as "awareness", which is common practice today, is a poor practice; there are many kinds of awareness but there is only one rigpa and besides, rigpa is substantially more than just awareness. Since this is such an important term and since it lacks an equivalent in English, I choose not to translate it.

This is the term used to indicate enlightened mind as experienced by the practitioner on the path of these practices. The term itself specifically refers to the dynamic knowing quality of mind. It absolutely does not mean a simple registering, as implied by the word "awareness" which unfortunately is often used to translate this term. There is no word in English that exactly matches it, though the idea of "seeing" or "insight on the spot" is very close. Proof of this is found in the fact that the original Sanskrit term "vidyā" is actually the root of all words in English that start with "vid" and mean "to see", for example, "video", "vision", and so on. Chogyam Trungpa Rinpoche, who was particularly skilled at getting Tibetan words into English, also stated that this term rigpa really did not have a good equivalent in English, though he thought that "insight" was the closest. My own conclusion after hearing extensive teaching on it is that rigpa is best left untranslated.

Samsara, Skt. saṃsāra, Tib. 'khor ba: This is the most general name for the type of existence in which sentient beings live. It refers to the fact that they continue on from one existence to another, always within the enclosure of births that are produced by ignorance and experienced as unsatisfactory. The original Sanskrit means to be constantly going about, here and there. The Tibetan term literally means "cycling", because of which it is frequently translated into English with "cyclic existence" though that is not quite the meaning of the term.

Shamatha, Skt. śhamatha, Tib. gzhi gnas: This is the name of one of the two main practices of meditation used in the Buddhist system to gain insight into reality. This practice creates a one-pointedness of mind which can then be used as a foundation for development of the insight of the other practice, vipaśhyanā.

Shine forth, shining forth, Tib. shar ba: This term means "to dawn" or "to come forth into visibility" either in the outer physical world or in the inner world of mind.

It is heavily used in texts on meditation to indicate the process of something coming forth into mind. There are other terms with this specific meaning but most of them also imply the process of dawning within a samsaric mind. "Shine forth" is special because it does not have that restricted meaning; it refers to the process of something dawning in any type of mind, un-enlightened and enlightened. It is an important term for the higher tantras of Mahāmudrā and Great Completion texts where there is a great need to refer to the simple fact of something dawning in mind especially in enlightened mind but also in un-enlightened mind.

In the Tibetan language, this term stands out and immediately conveys the meaning explained above. There are words in English like "to appear" that might seem easier to read than "shine forth", but they do not stand out and catch the attention sufficiently. Moreover, terms such as "appear" accurately translate other Tibetan terms which specifically indicate an un-enlightened context or a certain type of sensory appearance, so they do not convey the meaning of this term. There will be many times where this term's specific meaning of something occurring in any type of mind is crucial to a full understanding of the expression under consideration. For example, "shining-forth liberation" means that some content of mind, such as a thought, comes forth in either un-enlightened or enlightened mind, and that, on coming forth, is liberated there in that mind.

Spontaneous existence, Tib. lhun grub: Spontaneous existence is a key term in Essence Mahamudra and Nyingthig Great Completion. The term "grub" refers to something coming into existence. The term "lhun" means that it is happening spontaneously, though note that spontaneous here has the specific meaning of being without karmic cause and effect. Thus, spontaneous existence in these teachings has two, equally important connotations: presence as opposed to absence and a type of existence occurring of itself, outside the process of karmic cause and effect.

It is not correct to call this "spontaneous presence". The reason is rooted in the original Sanskrit term "siddhi" which is the standard term in that language for indicating the process of coming into existence. Presence merely indicates that something is present as opposed to absent; this term includes that sense but its main connotation is that there is a process of coming into existence, and that process is one which is not the karmic cause and effect process. There is also the issue that this term has both noun and verb forms. While one can talk about "spontaneously existing"or "spontaneously coming to exist" one cannot talk of "spontaneous presencing", and the like. Many translations of the texts using these terms have simply conflated the noun and verb forms into the noun form "spontaneous presence". In the process, most of the shades of meaning in this term—all of which are crucial to understanding this material— have been lost.

State, Tib. ngang: This is a key term in Mahāmudrā and Great Completion. Unfortunately it is often not translated and in so doing much meaning is lost. Alternatively, it is often translated as "within" which is incorrect. The term means a "state". A state is a certain, ongoing situation. In Buddhist meditation in general, there are various states that a practitioner has to enter and remain in as part of developing the meditation.

Superfact, Skt. paramārtha, Tib. don dam: This term is paired with the term "fictional" *q.v.* In the past, the terms have been translated as "relative" and "absolute" respectively, but those translations are nothing like the original terms. These terms are extremely important in the Buddhist teaching so it is very important that their translations be corrected but, more than that, if the actual meaning of these terms is not presented, the teaching connected with them cannot be understood.

The Sanskrit term literally means "the fact for that which is above all others, special, superior" and refers to the wisdom mind possessed by those who have developed themselves spiritually to the point of having transcended saṃsāra. That wisdom is *super*ior to an ordinary, un-developed person's consciousness and the *facts* that appear on its surface are superior compared to the facts that appear on the ordinary person's consciousness. Therefore, it is superfact or the holy fact, more literally. What this wisdom knows is true for the beings who have it, therefore what the wisdom sees is superfactual truth.

Superfice, superficies, Tib. rnam pa: In discussions of mind, a distinction is made between the entity of mind which is a mere knower and the superficial things that appear on its surface and which are known by it. In other words, the superficies are the various things which pass over the surface of mind but which are not mind. Superficies are all the specifics that constitute appearance—for example, the colour white within a moment of visual consciousness, the sound heard within an ear consciousness, and so on.

Suppression and furtherance, Tib. dgag sgrub: Suppression and furtherance is the term used to express the way that dualistic mind approaches the path to enlightenment. In that case, some states of mind are regarded as ones to be discarded, so the practitioner takes the approach of attempting to suppress or stop them, and some are regarded as ones to be developed, so the practitioner takes the approach of trying to go further with and develop them. These two poles represent the way that dualistic mind always works with itself. Thorough Cut practice goes beyond that duality.

The nature, Tib. rang bzhin: The nature is one of the three char-acteristics—of the core of mind entity, nature, and un-stopped compassionate activity. Using this term emphasizes that the empty entity does have a nature. In other words, its use explicitly shows that the core of mind is not merely empty. If you ask "Well, what is that nature like?" The answer is that it is luminosity, it is wisdom.

Thorough Cut, Tib. khregs chod: The innermost level of Great Completion has two main practices, the first called Thregcho which literally translates as Thorough Cut and the second called Thogal which translates as Direct Crossing. The meaning of Thorough Cut has been misunderstood. The meaning is clearly explained in the *Illuminator Tibetan-English Dictionary*:

> Thorough Cut is a practice that slices through the solidification produced by rational mind as it grasps at a perceived object and perceiving subject. It is done in order to get to the underlying reality which is always present in the core of mind and which is called Alpha Purity in this system of teachings. For this reason, Thorough Cut is also known as Alpha Purity Thorough Cut.

The etymology of the word is explained in the Great Completion teachings either as ཁྲེགས་སུ་ཆོད་པ་ or ཁྲེགས་གི་ཆོད་པ་. In either case, the term ཆོད་པ་ is "a cut"; there are all sorts of different "cuts" and this is one of them. Then, in the case of ཁྲེགས་སུ་ཆོད་པ་, ཁྲེགས་སུ་ is an adverb modifying the verb "to cut" and has the meaning of making the cut fully, completely. It is traditionally explained with the example of slicing off a finger. A finger could be sliced with a sharp knife such that the cut was not quite complete and the cut off portion was left hanging. Alternatively, it could be sliced through in one, decisive movement such that the finger was completely and definitely severed. That kind of thorough cut is what is meant here. In the case of ཁྲེགས་གི་ཆོད་པ་, the term ཁྲེགས་གི་ is an adverb that has the meaning of something that is doubtless, of something that is unquestionably so. A translation based on the first explanation would be "Thorough Cut" and on the second would be "Decisive Cut".

Other translations that have been put forward for this term are: "Cutting Resistance" and "Cutting Solidity". Both are grammatically incorrect. Further, the name "Cutting Resistance" is made on the basis of students expressing resistance to practice and the like, but that is not the meaning intended. Similarly, the name Cutting Solidity comes from not understanding that the term ཁྲེགས་ (khregs) has both old and new meanings; the newer meaning of "solid", "solidity" does not apply because the term Thorough Cut was put into use in the time of Padmasambhava when only the old meaning of ཁྲེགས་ was in use. The term means that the practitioner of this system cuts *decisively* through rational mind, regardless of its degree of solidity, so as to arrive directly at the essence of mind.

Unaltered or uncontrived, Tib. ma bcos pa: This term is the opposite of altered and contrived. It refers to something which has not been altered from its native state; something which has been left just as it is.

Unsatisfactoriness, Skt. duḥkha, Tib. sdug bngal: This term is usually translated into English with "suffering" but there are many problems with that. When the Buddha talked about the nature of samsaric existence, he said that it was unsatisfactory. He used the term "duḥkha", which includes actual suffering but means much more than that. Duḥkha is one of a pair of terms, the other being "sukha", which is usually translated as, but does not only mean, bliss. The real meaning of duḥkha is "everything on the side of bad"—not good, uncomfortable, unpleasant, not nice, and so on. Thus, it means "unsatisfactory in every possible way". The real meaning of its opposite, sukha, is "everything on the side of good"—not bad, comfortable, pleasant, nice, and so on.

Therefore, that he is completely liberated from the sufferings actually means that he has completely liberated himself from the unsatisfactoriness of saṃsāra, which includes all types of suffering and happiness, too.

Un-stopped, Tib. ma 'gags pa: An important path term in the teaching of both Mahāmudrā and Great Completion. The essence of mind has two parts: emptiness and luminosity. Both of these must come unified. However, when a practitioner does the practice, he will fall into one extreme or the other and that is called "stoppage". The aim of the practice is to get to the stage in which there is both emptiness and luminosity together. In that case, there is no stoppage of falling into one extreme or the other. Thus non-stopped luminosity is a term that indicates that there is the luminosity with all of its appearance yet that luminosity, for the practitioner, is not mistaken, is not stopped off. Stopped luminosity is an experience like luminosity but in which the appearances have, at least to some extent, not been mixed with emptiness.

Upadesha, Skt. upadeśa, Tib. man ngag: See under foremost instruction.

Vacillatory focus, Tib. gza' gtad: This term is twice pejorative. The word "vacillatory" refers to a process of hovering around a subject, seeing it from this angle and that angle because of vacillating over how it really is. "Focus" means that rational mind takes one of the possible angles and settles on that. For example, in the process of resting in the essence of mind, there can be the fault of not leaving rational mind but staying within in it and thinking, "Yes, this is the essence of mind" or "No, this is not it. It is that". Each of those is a vacillatory focus. Any vacillatory focus implies that the practitioner has not left rational mind and so is not in rigpa.

Vipashyana, Skt. vipaśyanā, Tib. lhag mthong: This is the Sanskrit name for one of the two main practices of meditation needed in the Buddhist system for gaining insight into reality. The other one, śhamatha, keeps the mind focussed while this one looks piercingly into the nature of things.

Wisdom, Skt. jñāna, Tib. ye shes: This is a fruition term that refers to the kind of mind—the kind of knower—possessed by a buddha. Sentient beings do have this kind of knower but it is covered over by a very complex apparatus for knowing, that is, dualistic mind. If they practise the path to buddha-hood, they will leave behind their obscuration and return to having this kind of knower.

The Sanskrit term has the sense of knowing in the most simple and immediate way. This sort of knowing is present at the core of every being's mind. Therefore, the Tibetans called it "the particular type of awareness which is there primordially". Because of the Tibetan wording it has often been called "primordial wisdom" in English translations, but that goes too far; it is just "wisdom" in the sense of the most fundamental knowing possible.

Wisdom does not operate in the same way as samsaric mind; it comes about in and of itself without depending on cause and effect. Therefore it is frequently referred to as "self-arising wisdom" *q.v.*

ABOUT THE AUTHOR,
PADMA KARPO TRANSLATION COMMITTEE,
AND THEIR SUPPORTS FOR STUDY

I have been encouraged over the years by all of my teachers to pass on the knowledge I have accumulated in a lifetime dedicated to study and practice, primarily in the Tibetan tradition of Buddhism. On the one hand, they have encouraged me to teach. On the other, they are concerned that, while many general books on Buddhism have been and are being published, there are few books that present the actual texts of the tradition. Therefore they, together with a number of major figures in the Buddhist book publishing world, have also encouraged me to translate and publish high quality translations of individual texts of the tradition.

My teachers always remark with great appreciation on the extraordinary amount of teaching that I have heard in this life. It allows for highly informed, accurate translations of a sort not usually seen. Briefly, I spent the 1970's studying, practising, then teaching the Gelugpa system at Chenrezig Institute, Australia, where I was a founding member and also the first Australian to be ordained as a monk in the Tibetan Buddhist tradition. In 1980, I moved to the United States to study at the feet of the Vidyadhara Chogyam Trungpa Rinpoche. I stayed in his Vajradhatu community, now called Shambhala, where I studied and practised all the Karma Kagyu, Nyingma, and Shambhala teachings being presented there and was a senior member of the Nalanda Translation Committee. After the vidyadhara's nirvana, I moved in 1992 to Nepal, where I have been continuously involved with the study, practise, translation, and teaching of the Kagyu system and especially of the Nyingma system of Great Completion. In recent years, I have spent extended times in Tibet with the greatest living Tibetan masters of Great Completion, receiving very pure transmissions of the ultimate levels of this teaching directly in Tibetan and practising them there in retreat. In that way, I have studied and practised extensively not in one Tibetan tradition as is usually done, but in three of the four Tibetan traditions—Gelug, Kagyu, and Nyingma—and also in the Theravada tradition, too.

With that as a basis, I have taken a comprehensive and long term approach to the work of translation. For any language, one first must have the lettering needed to write the language. Therefore, as a member of the Nalanda Translation Committee, I spent some years in the 1980's making Tibetan word-processing software and high-quality Tibetan fonts. After that, reliable lexical works are needed. Therefore, during the 1990's I spent some years writing the Illuminator Tibetan-English Dictionary and a set of treatises on Tibetan grammar, preparing a variety of key Tibetan reference works needed for the study and translation of Tibetan Buddhist texts, and giving our Tibetan software the tools needed to translate and research Tibetan texts. During this time, I also translated full-time for various Tibetan gurus and ran the Drukpa Kagyu Heritage Project—at the time the largest project in Asia for the preservation of Tibetan Buddhist texts. With the dictionaries, grammar texts, and specialized software in place, and a wealth of knowledge, I turned my attention in the year 2000 to the translation and publication of important texts of Tibetan Buddhist literature.

Padma Karpo Translation Committee (PKTC) was set up to provide a home for the translation and publication work. The committee focusses on producing books containing the best of Tibetan literature, and, especially, books that meet the needs of practitioners. At the time of writing, PKTC has published a wide range of books that, collectively, make a complete program of study for those practising Tibetan Buddhism, and especially for those interested in the higher tantras. All in all, you will find many books both free and for sale on the PKTC web-site. Most are available both as paper editions and e-books.

It would take up too much space here to present an extensive guide to our books and how they can be used as the basis for a study program. However, a guide of that sort is available on the PKTC web-site, whose address is on the copyright page of this book and we recommend that you read it to see how this book fits into the overall scheme of PKTC publications. In short, this book is about Thorough Cut. We have published many texts on the Thorough Cut teaching, each one carefully selected for its particular treatment of the subject. When studying the Thorough Cut teaching, the texts on the Three Lines teaching originally from Garab Dorje will be essential reading:

- *The Feature of the Expert, Glorious King* by Dza Patrul
- *About the Three Lines* by Dodrupchen III
- *Relics of the Dharmakaya* by Ontrul Tenpa'i Wangchug.

A few of the many other texts published by PKTC that deal with Thorough Cut and add further ornamentation are:

- *Flight of the Garuda* by Zhabkar
- *Empowerment and AtiYoga* by Tony Duff
- *Peak Doorways to Emancipation* by Shakya Shri
- *Alchemy of Accomplishment* by Dudjom Rinpoche
- *The Way of the Realized Old Dogs* by Ju Mipham
- *The Method of Preserving the Face of Rigpa* by Ju Mipham
- *Essential Points of Practice* by Zhechen Gyaltshab
- *Words of the Old Dog Vijay* by Zhechen Gyaltshab
- *Hinting at Dzogchen* by Tony Duff

The other main practice of Quintessential Dzogchen is Direct Crossing; other PKTC publications on Direct Crossing are:

- *Key Points of Direct Crossing called "Nectar of the Pure Part"* by Khenchen Padma Namgyal
- The most important text *Guidebook called "Highest Wisdom" (Triyig Yeshe Lama)* by Jigmey Lingpa.

We make a point of including, where possible, the relevant Tibetan texts in Tibetan script in our books. We also make them available in electronic editions that can be downloaded free from our web-site, as discussed below. The Tibetan text for this book is included at the back of the book.

Electronic Resources

PKTC has developed a complete range of electronic tools to facilitate the study and translation of Tibetan texts. For many years now, this software has been a prime resource for Tibetan Buddhist centres throughout the world, including in Tibet itself. It is available through the PKTC web-site. The wordprocessor TibetDoc has the only complete set of tools for creating, correcting, and formatting Tibetan text according to the norms of the Tibetan language. It can also be used to make texts with mixed Tibetan and English or other languages. Extremely high quality Tibetan fonts, based on the forms of Tibetan calligraphy learned from old masters from pre-Communist Chinese Tibet, are also available. Because of their excellence, these typefaces have achieved a legendary status amongst Tibetans.

TibetDoc is used to prepare electronic editions of Tibetan texts in the PKTC text input office in Asia. Tibetan texts are often corrupt so the input texts are carefully corrected prior to distribution. After that, they are made available through the PKTC web-site. These electronic texts are not careless productions like so many of the Tibetan texts found on the web, but are highly reliable editions useful to non-scholars and scholars alike. Some of the larger collections of these texts are for purchase, but most are available for free download.

The electronic texts can be read, searched, and even made into an electronic library using either TibetDoc or our other software, TibetD Reader. Like TibetDoc, TibetD Reader is advanced software with many capabilities made specifically to meet the needs of reading and researching Tibetan texts.

PKTC software is for purchase but we make a free version of TibetD Reader available for free download on the PKTC website.

A key feature of TibetDoc and Tibet Reader is that Tibetan terms in texts can be looked up on the spot using PKTC's electronic dictionaries. PKTC also has several electronic dictionaries—some Tibetan-Tibetan and some Tibetan-English—and a number of other reference works. The *Illuminator Tibetan-English Dictionary* is renowned for its completeness and accuracy.

This combination of software, texts, reference works, and dictionaries that work together seamlessly has become famous over the years. It has been the basis of many, large publishing projects within the Tibetan Buddhist community around the world for over thirty years and is popular amongst all those needing to work with Tibetan language or deepen their understanding of Buddhism through Tibetan texts.

TIBETAN TEXT

༄༅། །རྟོགས་ཚིགས་ཁྲིགས་ཆོད་ཀྱི་གདམས་པ་ཐུང་བསྲུབས་སློབ་མེའི་
སྐྱོང་བ་ཞེས་བྱ་བ་བཞུགས་སོ།།

༄༅། །གང་གི་རྡོ་རྗེས་ཕེག་མཚོག་རྟོགས་པ་ཅེའི། །ལམ་འདིར་རྒྱུ་
མཚོན་ཞེས་ནས་དང་ཐོབ་པ། །མཉམ་མེད་རྡོ་རྗེ་འཆང་དབང་བླ་མའི་
ཞབས། །བཏུད་ནས་སློམ་ཞེན་དགྱེས་པའི་མཆོད་འདི་སྐྱེད། །འདི་ན་
རྟོགས་ཅེན་སྨྲ་བ་མང་མོད་དེ། །ཁྲོག་འདིའི་ཤིང་ཏུ་ཀུན་མཁྱེན་སྐྱོང་ཅེན་
པའི། །རང་ལུགས་རེ་མོའི་མར་མེ་ལྟར་གྱུར་པས། །ཡང་དག་ལྟར་སྐྱོང་
བྱེད་པ་ཤིན་ཏུ་ཤུང་། །དེ་སྐྱོང་སྨྲ་བ་མང་ན་ཙོད་པའི་རྒྱུ། །མ་སྨྲ་བག་
ཡངས་སྤྱོད་པ་མཆོག་ཡིན་ཡང་། །ཆོས་དོན་གཉེར་བའི་ནན་ཏོ་མ་ལྟོག་
པས། །ཤུགས་འབྱུང་སྐྱོང་བ་འབྱུང་རྒྱལ་གཏུམ་ལབ་བྱ། །དབང་གྱུར་ལུ་
དང་རྣམ་དག་རིགས་པའི་མཐུས། །རྒྱུ་ཆེར་འཆད་ལའང་ཅུང་ཟད་དབང་མོད་
ཀྱི། །དེ་སྐྱོད་གནས་ལ་བསྐྱིལ་བ་ཐུང་དུའི་དགོ། །བསྒྲུས་ལ་དགའ་བའི་བློ་
དང་བསྐུན་ཏེ་འཆད། །དེ་ཡང་རྟོགས་ཅེན་མན་ངག་སྟེའི་ཤིང་ཏུ་ཅེན་པོ་

རྣམས་ཀྱི་བཞེད་པ་ལྟར་ན་ཆོས་འདི་སྟོང་རྗེ་བྲང་ཆུབ་ཀྱི་སེམས་ལ་བློ་སྦྱང་བ་
དང་། སྐྱ་ཐབལ་འགྱུར་ཆེན་པོ་ནས་བཤད་པའི་སྲོས་བཅས་དང་སྲོས་མེད་ལ་
སོགས་པའི་དབང་བཞི་རྟོགས་པར་ཐོབ་ནས་དག་ཆིག་ཆུལ་བཞིན་སྲུང་ནུས་པ་
དང་། ཁྱད་པར་དུ་ཡང་རྗེ་རྗེའི་ལམ་ཀྱི་ཉམས་རྟོགས་བཙན་ཐབས་སུ་འཆར་
བ་དོན་བརྒྱུད་དགོངས་པའི་བྱིན་རྣབས་འཕོ་བ་རག་ལས་པས་སློབ་དཔོན་སྦོ་དུ་མ་
ནས་མཉེས་པར་བྱེད་ནུས་པའི་སྲོད་ལྡན་ཀྱི་སློབ་མ་ཁོ་ན་ལ་སྟོན་པར་བཞེད་ཀྱི་
རྟེན་འབྲེལ་ཐོག་མ་ནས་འཆུག་པའི་ལམ་མགོ་མཐུག་མེད་པ་དུར་ཁྲོད་ཀྱི་མགལ་
བ་ལྟ་བུ་འདི་ནི་མི་བཞེད་དོ། །འདིའི་ཕྱིར་མཐའ་ཡས་པའི་སེམས་ཅན་ཐམས་
ཅད་བརྩག་པར་དགའར་བའི་སྲུག་བསྐུལ་ཀྱི་ཁྱུར་ཆེན་པོས་སྐད་ཆིག་རེ་རེ་བཞིན་དུ་
གཅོར་བ་འདི་ལ་ཁ་ཚོམ་མིན་པར་སྟོང་ཐག་པ་ནས་མ་བཟོད་པའི་སེམས་ཀྱིས་
དུས་རྒྱུ་ཆོད་སུ་ཕྱིར་ཡང་རྟོགས་བྱུང་ཐོབ་པ་ལ་ཡིད་རིངས་པ་ཞིག་གིས་ལམ་
འདི་ལ་བརྟེན་ནས་ཚེ་གཅིག་ལུས་གཅིག་པོ་འདིའི་སྟེང་ནས་འཛིན་ལུས་འཕོ་བ་
ཆེན་པོའི་ཡེ་ཤེས་ཀྱི་སྐུ་བསྒྲུབས་ཏེ་སེམས་ཅན་མ་ལུས་པ་འཁོར་བ་ལས་སྒྲོལ་
བའི་དེད་དཔོན་གཅིག་པུར་འགྱུར་ནུས་པ་དེ་བས་ན་ཐེག་མཆོག་རྒྱལ་པོ་ཞེས་བྱ་
བའི་མིང་གྲགས་སྐལ་ཚམ་དུ་མ་ལུས་པར་མཐོང་ངོ་། །ཁོ་འཕང་དེ་ལྟ་བུ་
སྒྲུབ་པ་ལ་ཟབ་པ་ཁྲིགས་ཆོད་དང་རྒྱ་ཆེ་བ་ཐོད་རྒྱལ་ཀྱི་ལམ་གཉིས་བྱུང་འབྲེལ་དུ་
ཉམས་སུ་བླངས་ནས་ཉམས་སྐྱོང་མཐར་དབྱུང་བ་ཞིག་དགོས་ལ། དེའི་ནང་
ནས་ཀྱང་སྐྱོབ་རེམ་ཀྱི་དང་པོ་ཁྲིགས་ཆོད་ནས་འཐུག་དགོས་པས་འདིར་རེ་ཞིག
དེ་བཤད་པར་བྱ་སྟེ། དེ་ལ་ཁྲིགས་ཆོད་ཅེས་པའི་མཚན་དོན་ནི། ཤེས་རབ་
ཀྱི་ཕར་ཕྱིན་བསྒོམས་པའི་མཐུ་ལས་གྲུང་དང་འཛིན་པའི་སྡུང་བ་ཐད་ཀར་
གཅོད་པ་ལ་སྐྱ་ཐབལ་འགྱུར་ནས་གསུངས་ཤིང་། སྐྱབས་འདིའི་ཤེར་ཕྱིན་ནི་
སེམས་དང་རིག་པ་གཉིས་ཀྱི་རྣམས་ཕྱེ་བའི་རིག་པ་ཡིན་ལུགས་ཀྱི་ལྟ་བ་ཕུ་ཐག

ཆོད་པའི་ས་ནས་སྐྱེད་པ་དེའོ། །རིག་པ་དེ་ཉོ་འཕྲོད་ཕན་ཆད་སེམས་མ་བཅོས་

པར་སྐྱོང་བའི་བཤག་ཐབས་ཁོ་ནས་གནས་ལུགས་ཀྱི་རང་ཞལ་ལྟ་བ་མ་གཏོགས་

འདི་བྱ་དང་འདི་སྒོམ་གྱི་སྒོས་པའི་དམིགས་གཏད་ཕྱ་མོ་ཡང་དགོས་རྒྱུ་མེད་མོད།

ཅོན་ཀྱང་དེའི་སྔོན་དུ་ཏོ་སྒྱིང་སྒྲུབ་པའི་རྒྱུད་ལས་གསུངས་པའི་རིམ་འཛུག་གི་ངོ་

སྒྱིད་འདི་ཡང་རེས་པར་དགོས་ཏེ། །འདི་སྔོན་དུ་མ་སོང་ན་ཆོས་ཉིད་ཀྱི་

བཤགས་ཚུལ་རྗེན་པར་མཐོང་བ་དཀའ་འོ། །གདུལ་བྱ་ཆོ་སྲ་མ་ལ་ལས་

འདིར་རྒྱུད་སྒྲུངས་པའི་གང་ཟག་གཅིག་ཡིན་ན་ནི་ཏོ་སྒྱིང་གི་གོ་རིམ་འདི་ལྟར་

བྱེད་དགོས་པའི་ཁྱབ་མཐའ་མེད་ཀྱི་དེ་དང་གཞན་མི་འདུའོ། །དེས་ན་ཏོ་སྒྱིང་

འདི་ལ་གསུམ། །སྣང་བ་སེམས་སུ་ཏོ་སྒྲུད་དེ་ད་ལྟ་རང་རེ་རྣམས་ལ་ཡུལ་

སྣང་ཕྱི་དོན་དུ་འཆར་བ་འདི་རྣལ་འབྱོར་པའི་ནང་སེམས་ཀྱི་སྣང་ཆ་ཚམ་དུ་མཐོང་

བ་དང་། །སེམས་ཉིད་སྒྱིང་པར་ཏོ་སྒྲུད་དེ་འཛིན་པ་རང་མཚན་ལྟར་སྣང་བ

འདི་ཡང་དོན་དམ་པར་ན་གྲུབ་པའི་དངོས་པོ་ཅུང་ཟད་ཀྱང་མེད་པར་མཐོང་བ

དང་། །སྒྱིང་པ་རིག་པ་ཏོ་སྒྲུད་དེ་ཀུན་རྫོབ་ཀྱི་སྣང་བ་ཡུལ་དང་ཡུལ་ཅན་

ཐམས་ཅད་བདེན་མེད་སྒྱུ་མ་དང་སྐྲི་ལམ་གྱི་འཆར་སྒོ་ལྟར་མཐོང་བ་ལ་བསླབ

པར་བྱ་བ་སྟེ། །གང་ཟག་གི་རིགས་ཁ་ཅིག་དེ་ཁོ་ན་ཉིད་ལ་རིམ་གྱིས་བཀྲི་བའི

ཐབས་མཁས་ཀྱི་སྒོ་གཅིག་གོ །འིན་ཀྱང་མཐར་ཕུག་གི་དོན་ལ་སྣང་བ

སེམས་སུ་ཏོ་སྒྲུད་པ་ཡང་བདེན་ཞེན་གྱིས་བཏང་བ་མིན་པར་དཔལ་ལྡན་ཟླ་བའི

ཞབས་དང་ཀུན་མཁྱེན་སྐྱོང་ཆེན་པའི་བཞེད་པ་ལྟར་ཐམས་ཅད་མཁྱེན་པ་འཇིགས

མེད་གླིང་པས་ཀྱང་རྒྱལ་དུ་བཏོན་ནས་བཤད་དེ། །ཤེས་དང་ཤེས་བྱ་བདེན་རྫུན

གྱི་རྣམ་དབྱེ་མི་འདུ་བར་འཐད་པ་མིན་པའི་ཕྱིར་རོ། །དེ་བས་ན་ཁམས་གསུམ

ལ་སོགས་པའི་སྣང་བ་ཐམས་ཅད་རྟོག་པའི་རང་མདངས་དང་རིག་པའི་རྩལ

ཤུགས་ཚམ་ལས་ཡུལ་དང་ཡུལ་ཅན་རང་རང་གི་སྟེང་ནས་སྐྱེད་རྒྱུ་ཞིག་གཏན

ནས་མེད་པས་ཤེས་བྱ་ལ་སྒྲིབ་སྟེ་ཤེས་པ་དང་ཤེས་པ་ལ་སྒྲིབ་ནས་ཤེས་བྱ་ཞེས་
བཏགས་པའི་ཐ་སྙད་ཀྱི་ཧྲུན་རིས་ཁོ་ནར་མཆོང་རྟོག །དེ་ལ་བརྟེན་ནས་ཡོད་
མེད་ཡིན་མིན་ལ་སོགས་པའི་མཐར་འཛིན་གྱི་འཆིང་བ་དྲལ་ཙམ་ཡང་མ་
དགྲིགས་པའི་འོད་གསལ་སྟོང་པ་ཉིད་ཀྱི་དབྱིངས་སོ་སོ་རང་གིས་རིག་པར་བྱ་བ་
དེ་གཞན་ཤེར་གྱི་རྟེས་བརྗོད་ཁོ་ནས་ཡོད་གང་བ་མ་ཡིན་པར་ངེས་ཤེས་ཕུ་ཐག་
ཆོད་པར་བྱ་སྟེ། འདི་གཉིས་ཀ་རྒྱུད་ཀྱི་དགོངས་པའི་ཕྱོགས་རེ་རེར་ཁས་བླང་
ངོ། །དེ་ནས་དངོས་གཞིའི་དོ་སྦྱོར་ནི། སྤྱིར་དཔེ་དོན་སྦྱར་བའི་དོ་སྦྱོར་
ཉེར་གཅིག་སོགས་མང་དུ་གསུངས་ཀྱང་སྐབས་འདིའི་དོ་སྦྱོར་གྱི་མན་འགག་
སེམས་རིག་ཤན་འབྱེད་ལ་ཐུག་པར་གཟིགས་ནས་ཀུན་མཁྱེན་རྣམ་པ་གཉིས་ཀས་
ཆུལ་འདི་སྟོ་དུ་མ་ནས་གཏན་ལ་ཕབ་སྟེ་བཤད་མོད། འོད་གསལ་གྱི་རྒྱུད་དོ་
སྟོད་སྐྱས་པ་སོགས་ནས་གནས་དང་སྟོ་དང་བཞུགས་ཆུལ་ལ་སོགས་པས་
སེམས་རིག་གི་ཁྱད་པར་ཞིབ་ཏུ་གསུང་བ་ལ་བལྟ་ཏོག་ཆུང་ཞིང་རྒྱུད་དོན་མན་
ངག་གིས་ཕྱེ་བའི་བཀའ་དྲིན་ལ་མི་སེམས་པ་ཚོས་སེམས་དང་རིག་པའི་ཤན་
འབྱེད་ཀྱི་འཕྱོང་ཤེར་རྒྱ་ཞིག་སྟོན་གྱི་ལོ་པཆ་རྣམས་ལ་མ་གྲགས་ཀྱང་རིག་འཛིན་
འཇིགས་སྦྱིང་གིས་རང་བཟོ་ཡིན་ཞེས་ཤེར་བ་ནི་ཁ་བདུད་ཀྱིས་བསྐུལ་བའི་སྟེ་
སྤྲགས་ཤིག་ཐེག་པའི་རྒྱལ་པོའི་གྲུབ་མཐའ་ལ་ཐན་སྐྱེལ་དུ་འོང་བ་ཁོ་ནར་ཟད་དེ།
དེ་ལ་སེམས་ཞེས་བྱ་བ་ནི། ད་ལྟའི་ཐ་མལ་གྱི་རྣམ་རྟོག་དགར་སྤྲག་དང་རེ་
དོགས་ལ་སོགས་པའི་རྣམ་པ་གཞན་དང་གཞན་དུ་འགྱུར་བའི་མཚན་ཉིད་ཅན་འདི་
དང་། སྣོ་ལྟའི་ཤེས་པ་གཟུང་ཡུལ་ལ་འཐུག་པ་རྣམས་ཏེ། འདི་དང་འདིའི་
ཕྱོགས་གཏོགས་འཁྲོ་གནས་ཀྱི་ཤེས་རྣམས་ཐམས་ཅད་ལས་རླུང་གི་བཞོན་པ་ཅན་
ལས་མ་འདས་པར་དུ་ལོང་བ་ཀཏང་ཅན་དང་མི་འཕྱི་པོ་མིག་ལྡན་གཉིས་ཆོགས་
པའི་དཔེས་སེམས་ཡུལ་ཐོག་ཏུ་གཡོ་བ་དང་། །ཡུལ་འཛིན་པ་གཉིས་ཀྱི་བྱེད་

ལས་རྒྱུང་རྨྱུང་སེམས་ཚོགས་པའི་ནུས་མཐུར་ཀུན་མཁྱེན་གཞིས་པས་བཤད་དེ། །

རྒྱུད་སྨུ་ཏིག་ཕྲེང་བ་ལ་སོགས་པར་སྒྲིང་ང་སྐྲེང་སྒྲང་གི་བདག་པོ་རྨྱང་དུ་བཤད་པ་

ཡང་འདི་འདུ་བའི་དོན་མང་པོ་ཞིག་ལ་དགོངས་ནས་ཡིན་ནོ། །སེམས་དེ་ངོས་

ཟིན་པ་གཅིག་པུས་མི་ཚོག་པས་ད་དུང་ཞིག་ཏུ་དཔྱད་ན་འཁོར་བ་ཐོག་མ་མེད་པ་

ནས་མ་རིག་པའི་རྣམ་རྟོག་སྟོབས་སུ་གྱུར་ཅིང་། །རང་རྒྱུད་ལ་ལས་ཀྱི་བཞག་

པའི་བག་ཆགས་ཡོངས་སུ་སྨྲིན་ནས་ཏེར་ལེན་གྱི་ཕུང་པོའི་སྟེང་དུ་བདེ་བ་དང་

སྡུག་བསྔལ་བྱིས་པའི་རྡོལ་ཐབས་བཞིན་དུ་འབྱུང་ཞིང་། །དེའི་རྟེས་ལ་དེ་ལྟར་

ཞེན་པའི་སེམས་འབྱུང་བས་མཚོན་ཏེ་ཟག་བཅས་ཀྱི་གནས་ལུས་ལོངས་སྤྱོད་ལ་

སོགས་པ་འབྱུལ་སྲུང་ཐ་མལ་དུ་ཞེན་པའི་སེམས་ཀྱི་རྒྱུ་བ་ཇི་སྲིད་པ་ཐམས་ཅད་

རྒྱུ་ཀྱེན་སྐྱོ་བྱུར་བའི་དབང་གིས་འབྱུལ་པ་ཉིད་འབྱུལ་དུ་ཕར་ནས་རང་སྲུང་ལ་

གཞན་དུ་བྱུང་བ་མ་གཏོགས་སེམས་ཀྱི་གཤིས་ལ་འབྱུལ་སྲུང་གིས་བསྒྱུར་བའི་

ཚོས་མདོག་དེ་ལྟ་བུ་ཞིག་ཡོད་རྒྱུད་མི་འདུག་སྐྱམ་དུ་ལེགས་པར་ཙུད་བཅད།

དེའང་དཔེ་མའི་མན་ངག་དང་བྲལ་བའི་གང་ཟག་རྣམས་ལ་སྐྱོ་བྱུར་གྱི་ཡུལ་དང་

བཅས་པའི་སེམས་འདི་ལས་ལྷག་པའི་ཡེ་ཤེས་གཞན་ཞིག་ད་ལྟ་ནས་རོ་འཕྲོད་པ་

མེད་ཀྱང་། །ཐེག་པ་འདིའི་ལུགས་ལ་ནི་དེ་འདུ་བའི་ནང་གི་ཡེ་ཤེས་སེམས་

ཅན་ཐམས་ཅད་ཀྱི་རྒྱུད་ལ་གཟོད་མ་ནས་འབྱལ་མ་སྨྱོང་བའི་ཚོས་སྐྱེའི་རང་ཞལ་

རྟེན་པ་ཞིག་ཨ་མའི་མན་ངག་གིས་བསྐུན་རྒྱུ་ཡོད་དེ། །དེ་ངོ་ཤེས་ན་ཐེག་པ་

གཞན་གྱི་ལྟག་མཐོང་བསྐལ་པ་མང་པོར་བསྒོམ་པ་ལས་ཀྱང་ལམ་འདིའི་མཉམ་

བཞག་ཐུན་གཅིག་ས་ཚོད་ཆེ་བའི་གནད་ཟབ་མོ་ཡོད་དོ། །ཡེ་ཤེས་དེའི་

བཞགས་ཚུལ་རོ་འཕྲོད་པའི་སྒོ་ཡང་མདོར་བསྡུ་ན་གསུམ་སྟེ། །དོ་བོ་སྟོང་

པར་བཞགས་པས་དགའ་སྒྲུབ་ཆེན་འརྫིན་ལ་མ་ལྟོས་པར་ཡིན་དགྱོད་ཀྱི་འཆིང་བ་

རྫལ་ཚམ་ཡང་དོ་བོའི་སྟེང་ན་ཡོད་མ་སྨྱོང་སྟེ་དོ་རྗེ་ནམ་མཁའི་སྒྲོང་ཆེན་ལྟ་བུ།

རང་བཞིན་གསལ་བར་བཤགས་པས་བསལ་བཞག་སྨྲོ་བསྐུལ་མ་ལྩོས་པར་བྱིང་

འཐིབས་ཀྱི་མུན་པ་ཆ་ཚམ་ཡང་གཤིས་ཀྱི་སྙིང་ན་འཁྲུག་མ་མྱོང་བས་འོད་གསལ་

ཉི་མའི་དཀྱིལ་འཁོར་པ་ལྷ་བུ། ཐུགས་རྗེ་ཀུན་ཁྱབ་ཏུ་བཤགས་པས་བུ་རྩོལ་

གྱི་ངལ་བ་ལ་མ་ལྩོས་པར་འབྱུལ་གྲོལ་ཐབས་ཅད་གཅིག་མའི་རང་རྩལ་ལས་

གཞན་དུ་གྲུབ་མ་མྱོང་བས་གཉིད་མོ་ཆེའི་སྐྲི་ལམ་ལྟ་བུ་སྟེ། རིག་པའི་ངོ་བོ་

ལ་ཀ་དག་གི་བཤགས་ཚུལ་དེ་ལྷ་བུ་ཡོད་པས་འབྲས་བུ་རྣམ་པར་མི་རྟོག་པ་ཆོས་

སྐུའི་ཡེ་ཤེས་གདལ་ཁྱབ་སྟོང་པ་ཉིད་ཀྱི་རྣམ་པ་ཅན་འགྲུབ་པའི་གོ་འབྱེད།

རིག་པའི་རང་བཞིན་ལ་ལྷུན་གྲུབ་ཀྱི་གསལ་ཆ་དེ་ལྷ་བུ་ཡོད་པས་འབྲས་བུ་རྣམ་

པ་ཐམས་ཅད་པ་ལོངས་སྐུའི་ཡེ་ཤེས་གསལ་མདངས་འགགས་པ་མེད་པའི་རྣམ་

པ་ཅན་འཆར་བའི་གོ་འབྱེད། རིག་པའི་རང་རྩལ་ལ་ཀུན་ཁྱབ་ཀྱི་ཐུགས་རྗེ་དེ་

ལྷ་བུ་ཡོད་པས་འབྲས་བུ་རོལ་པ་སྣ་ཚོགས་པ་སྒྱུལ་སྐུའི་ཡེ་ཤེས་གང་འདུལ་དེར་

སྣང་གི་རྣམ་པ་ཅན་འབྱུང་བའི་གོ་འབྱེད། དེ་ལྟར་གདོད་མའི་ཡེ་གཞི་སྟོང་པ་

ལ་ཕུལ་ཆད་མེན་པ། བདེ་བ་ལ་ཞེན་པ་མེད་པ། གསལ་བ་ལ་རྟོག་པས་མ་

གོས་པ་རྣལ་ལོ། ཞིང་དེ། ཡེར་རེ། མཚན་ཉིད་གཞན་དུ་མི་འགྱུར་

བར་རིན་པོ་ཆེ་གསེར་གྱི་ཁམས་ལྟར་བཞུགས་ཀྱང་ཐ་མལ་བའི་སྣྲོ་གསུམ་བག་

ཆགས་དང་བཅས་པའི་སྒྲིབས་སུ་འཐུམས་ཏེ་རང་ངོ་རང་གིས་མ་མཐོང་བའི་ཆ

ནས་ནད་གསལ་གཞིན་དུ་བུམ་པའི་སྒུ་ཞེས་བདགས་པ་ཡིན་ནོ། དེ་རང་ཐོག་

ཏུ་སྟོང་ལུགས་འདིའི་སྟེང་ནས་འཁྲུག་ན་ཐག་གཅིག་ཐོག་ཏུ་གཏོང་པ་དང་

གདེངས་གྲོལ་ཐོག་ཏུ་བཅའ་བའང་དེའི་རྗེས་སུ་སློགས་འགྲོ་བས་ཤིན་ཏུ་གཟབ་

པར་བྱ་ལ། དེ་སྟོང་ལུགས་ཀྱང་དགེ་རྩ་ཡོངས་སུ་སྨིན་པའི་གང་ཟག་འགའ་

ཞིག་ལ་བྱིན་རླབས་བཅན་ཐབས་སུ་འཕོ་བའི་སློབས་ཀྱིས་དབང་དུས་ལ་སོགས་

པར་ཡེ་ཤེས་དེ་འཕྲོད་པའང་ཡོད་མོད་ཀྱི། སྤྱིར་བཏང་ནི་བརྫ་ཐབས་གཏན

ཚོགས་དུ་མས་ཡིན་ལུགས་ཀྱི་དོ་པོ་ཕུ་ཐག་ཆོད་པར་བཤད་ནས་སྒྲོབ་པའི་རྒྱུད་

ལ་གོ་བ་ཁྱུང་པར་ཐན་སྐྱེ་རེས་སུ་ཐུས་པ་དེ་དགོས་ཤིང་། གོ་བ་དེའི་སྟེང་ནས་

ཇེ་སྙེད་སྒོམ་བྱུང་གི་མྱོང་བ་མ་སྐྱེས་ཀྱི་བར་དུ་རང་ཉིད་ཀྱིས་བརྟོན་འགྲུས་ཆེན་

པོས་ཉམས་ལེན་སྒྲོང་ཆུལ་ལ་སྒྲོབ་དགོས་པ་ཡིན་གྱིས། ཕླ་སྒོམ་ཡིན་སྣམ་

ལ་བཞག་པ་གཅིག་པུས་མི་ཚོག་གོ། མཛོར་ན་སྐབས་འདིའི་སེམས་དང་ཡེ་

ཤེས་ཞེས་པ་ནི་གཞུང་ལུགས་ཕལ་ལ་གྲགས་པའི་སེམས་དང་ཡེ་ཤེས་ཀྱི་བརྡ་

ཆད་དང་བསྲེ་མི་རུང་བའི་ཟབ་གནད་ཕུན་མོང་མ་ཡིན་པ་ཡོད་ལ། ཡེ་ཤེས་དེ་

མཛོན་དུ་བྱེད་པའང་སེམས་ཅན་ཐ་མལ་པ་རྣམས་འཆི་བའི་དུས་སུ་ལས་རླུང་མ་

ལུས་པ་དབུ་མའི་དབྱིངས་སུ་བསྡུས་པ་ལ་བརྟེན་ནས་ཀུན་ཏུ་བཟང་པོའི་རིག་པ་

ཟང་ཐལ་ཕྱི་ནང་མེད་པའི་ཆུལ་དུ་དར་གཅིག་སྐྱང་ཡང་དོས་མི་ཟིན་པ་ཡིན།

རྣལ་འབྱོར་པས་ནི་ད་ལྟ་བཞག་ཐབས་ཀྱི་གདམས་ངག་ལ་བརྟེན་ནས་མཛོན་དུ་

བྱེད་ལུགས་ཤིག་ཡོད་དེ། དེ་ཇེ་ལྟར་ཡིན་ན། འཕད་མ་ཐག་པའི་ཡེ་ཤེས་

ཀྱི་རང་དོ་དེ་ཆུལ་བཞིན་དུ་ཆོས་ཉིད་མ་བཅོས་པའི་དན་པའི་སྟེང་ནས་སྒྲོང་ཤེས་

ན་རྒྱལ་གྱི་རྣམ་རྟོག་ཆགས་སྐྱང་གངི་མུག་གི་ཆར་གྱུར་པ་ཐམས་ཅད་སྒྲིན་ནས་

མ་ཁའི་དང་དུ་བབ་ལ་ཞ་བ་ལྟར་དེ་ས་ནས་རིག་པའི་དོ་པོ་ཇེ་གསལ་ལ་དུ་འོང་བ་

ཡིན་ནོ། ༈ འི་ན་ཡེ་ཤེས་ཀྱི་དོ་པོ་དན་པས་སྒྲོང་ལུགས་དེ་གང་ཡིན་སྣམ་ན།

འདི་ལ་བཞག་ཐབས་བདུན་དང་གྲོལ་ལུགས་གསུམ་ལ་སོགས་པ་མང་པོ་ཞིག

འབྱུང་ཡང་། དོན་བསྡུས་ན། སྤུར་དོ་སྒྱེད་པའི་རིག་པ་དེ་ཉིད་ད་ལྟའི་རྣམ་

རྟོག་ཐ་མལ་པ་འདི་ཀའི་དོད་པོར་བཞག་ནས་དེའི་དོ་པོ་སྐྱད་ཅིག་གྱུང་མ་བརྟེད་

པར་དན་པས་རྒྱུན་སྐྱོང་ཞིང་། དེ་རང་དན་བྱུ་དང་དན་བྱེད་འབེན་དང་མདའ་ཕླ་

བུའི་གཟབ་གཏད་ཅན་མ་ཡིན་པ་གཤུག་མའི་རང་ཞལ་མ་བོར་བ་ཙམ་གྱིས་ཚོག

ཤེས་པར་བྱས་ནས་སྒློ་བ་དེ་ལ་གུ་ཡངས་པ་ཞིག་གི་ངང་ནས་གཟུང་འཛིན་གྱི

འཁུལ་པ་ཐད་ཀར་འཇིག་རྱས་པ་སྟེ། རྟོག་པ་གང་ཞར་གྱི་སྨྲ་འགགས་གུང་ས་འདེབས་པ་ཚམ་མ་ཡིན་པར་རྣམ་རྟོག་འཁར་མཁན་གྱི་རྟེ་བོ་ལ་ཅེར་གྱི་བལྟ་ཞིས་སྟོམ་ཆེན་པ་དག་སྨྲ་བཞང་རྟོ་རྗེ་འདི་ཉིད་ལ་བཙལ་དགོས་སོ། །སྨོམ་བྱེད་པ་ལ་རྣམས་ཀྱི་གོགས་མེལ་ཀུང་ཞེས་དགོས་པ་མང་པོ་ཡོད་མོ་ད། ཞེན་གུང་གཙོ་བོར་བྱེད་སྐྱོད་གཚད་པ་ལ་མཁས་ན་གོགས་མེལ་ཕལ་ཆེར་དེའི་ནང་དུ་ཚང་བས། འདི་ལ་སེམས་ད་ཅང་བཙངས་པ་དག་ནས་ཞེས་རིག་གི་ངར་ཆག་པ་དང་། སྐྱོད་པ་དག་ནས་སེམས་རང་ཚུགས་མ་ཟིན་པའི་བྱེད་རྣམས་གཉིས་དང་། འགྱུ་བ་རྒྱུ་རྣབས་ལྦར་ཡུལ་ཐོག་ཏུ་གཡོ་བའི་འཕྲོ་རྟོད་རྣམས་ལས་བྱེད་བ་གཙོད་པ་ནི། སྨྱག་བཙོར་ཨ་འཐབས་ཀྱི་དྱན་པས་སེམས་གཅུར་བ་ལྦུ་མ་ཡིན་པར་ཤུགས་བྱང་རང་བབས་ཀྱི་དྱན་པ་སོ་མའི་ངར་ཐོགས་ནས་རིག་པ་ཧུར་བཏོན་ནས་བསྒོམ་པ་ཉིད་ཀྱིས་འགྱུབ་ཅིང་། འཕྲོ་རྟོད་གཙོད་པ་འང་གནས་དགའ་འགྱུ་སྐྱག་གི་རྟོག་པ་ཉིད་འཁུལ་དུ་འབྱམས་པ་ལས་ཆེས་འཕགས་པ་འགྱུ་བའི་ཡལ་ས་མཐར་ཤུག་གི་སྟེང་དུ་བློའི་འཇག་པ་ཐམས་ཅད་རོ་གཅིག་པར་བསྱེས་ནས་བཞག་པས་དེ་ལས་གཞན་པའི་ཆེ་ཤར་དང་ཆེ་སྱང་ཐམས་ཅད་ཆོས་སྐུའི་རོལ་རྩལ་དུ་བུན་ཞིག་གིས་འཁར་བ་མ་གཏོགས་མཚམ་བཞག་འཕོག་རྱས་ཀྱི་གོགས་སུ་འབྱུང་མི་སྱིད་པས་རང་གྲོལ་ཕྱོགས་རིས་ལས་འདས་པའི་རྟོགས་པ་གདེངས་སུ་གྱུར་པ་སྟེ། འདི་ནི་གནས་ཆ་བཏན་པོ་རྗེད་པའི་ཞི་གནས་ཀྱི་ཤེས་རྣམས་ཐུན་མོང་བ་འགན་ཞིག་ལ་བརྟེན་ནས་རྣམ་རྟོག་ཐམས་ཅད་ཆོས་སྐུ་ཡིན་ཟེར་བ་ཚོ་དང་ཡང་ཤིན་ཏུ་མི་མཚུངས་ཏེ། རྒྱ་ཆེར་ཆོས་དབྱིངས་མཛོད་འགྲོལ་ལ་བལྟས་པས་ཤེས་སོ། །དེའི་ཕྱིར་བཞག་ཐབས་སྐྱོན་མེད་གཅིག་ཤེས་ན་དེ་ཁོ་ནའི་མཐུས་བྱེད་སྐྱོད་ཚོད་པ་དགོས་ཀྱི། བྱི་མང་གིས་དུབ་དུས་གཅིག་ལ་ཁ་བསྔས་ན་གཞན་ཀྱིས་རྒྱབ་ནས་འདྲ་བ་ལྦ་བུའི་

གེགས་སེལ་ལ་སྙིང་པོ་མེད་དོ། །མདོར་ན་མན་ངག་གི་གནད་ཟབ་མོ་འགག།
བརྒྱ་ཆེངས་གཅིག་གིས་བསྒྲུམས་པ་མ་མཐོང་བར་སྐོམ་མེད་དང་། །ཁྱབ་
གདལ་ལ་སོགས་ཆོས་སྐད་ཚོན་པོ་གོ་ན་ལ་མཐོ་རྣབ་ཤེས་པ་ཙམ་གྱིས་ས་བཅད་
པ་ཙི་ཡང་མེད་པས་དེ་སྐྱོད་དང་བཞག་ཐབས་སྙིང་པོའི་དོན་ལ་མཁས་པར་བྱའོ།
རྣམས་སྐྱོང་རང་གི་རྒྱུད་ལ་མི་མཚེ་ཡང་། །བརྒྱུད་ལྡན་བླ་མའི་མན་ངག་མང་
ཐོས་པས། །མ་མཐོང་མཐོང་འདུའི་དག་སྐོས་གཅོང་མ་བརྒྱ། །ལྱུང་ལྱུང་
འབབ་པའི་མགྲིན་པ་ཆོས་ཀྱི་དུད། །དེ་སྐྱད་བྱུན་པོ་རང་གཅིགས་ཆེ་བ
དང་། །མཁས་རྟོམས་རྟོག་གེའི་སྐེམས་པས་བསྐྱིང་བ་ཡི། །འཆལ་
གཏམ་མ་འདྲེས་སྟོན་བྱུང་རིག་འཛིན་གྱི། །གསུང་རྒྱུན་ཡི་གེར་བཀོད་ལ།
སྐྱོན་ཡོད་མིན། གོ་སྐྲ་ཏུང་དུར་བརྗོད་པའི་བྱེའུ་མིག་འདི། །བཟུང་ནས་
ཀུན་མཁྱེན་གསུང་རབ་སྐྱོ་བཀྲའི་ལུགས། །རྣམ་པར་ཕྱེ་སྟེ་སྐྱབ་པ་ནན་ཏན་
གྱིས། །ཏིག་གས་པའི་ཁྱད་རོར་ལག་ཏུ་ལོངས་པར་མཛོད། །དེ་ལྱར་ཟབ
དོན་མན་ངག་སྙིང་པོའི་གཏམ། །བརྗོད་པའི་དགེ་འདིས་མཐའ་ཀླས་ཡིད་ཅན་
ཀུན། །རྡོ་རྗེ་རྗེ་མོའི་གསེང་ལམ་ལ་བརྟེན་ནས། །ཁྱད་ཆོས་དྲུག་ལྡན་
དབྱིངས་སུ་འཚང་རྒྱ་ཤོག །ཅེས་པའང་གནམ་དུ་འགོད་པའི་ཡོངས་འཛིན་བཤེན་གཉེན
དལ་པ་བློ་གྲོས་བཟང་པོས་རེ་དང་མོ་ནས་བསྐུལ་ཞིང་། ཉེ་ཆར་སྐྲབ་པ་ནན་ཏན་ལ་གསས་པའི་བཙུན་
པ་དྷ་མ་གྱི་ནས་ཀྱང་བསྐུལ་བ་ལྱར་མདོ་ཁམས་ཀྱི་སྒྲུང་སྐྱེན་ཆོས་སྐྲ་བའི་གཟུགས་བརྒྱན་འཛིགས་
མེད་བསྐུན་པའི་ཉི་མས་ཡར་ལུང་བཀྲ་བཀོང་གི་སྐྲབ་སྟེར་སྦྱར་བ་ཕྱོགས་དུས་ཐམས་ཅད་དུ་དགེ་ཞིང་
བཀྲ་ཤིས།། དགེའོ། །དགེའོ། དགེའོ།།

INDEX

CPSIA information can be obtained at www.ICGtesting.com
Printed in the USA
BVOW03s0640170314

347781BV00001B/8/P

9 789937 572699